# YOUR SAFE SPACE

Creating A Home Where
Autistic Children Thrive

Jo Gaunt

Copyright © 2024 Jo Gaunt

First published in Great Britain in 2024
Independently Published

Jo Gaunt asserts the moral right to be identified as the author of this work in accordance with the Copyright, Designs and Patents Act 1988.

ISBN 9798333730664 (Paperback)
ISBN 9798333747877 (Hardback)
All rights reserved.

No part of this book may be reproduced or transmitted in any form or by any means, electronic or mechanical, including photocopying, recording, or by any information storage and retrieval system without the written permission of the author, except where permitted by law or for the use of brief quotations in a book review.

The content provided in this book is based on the author's personal experiences and opinions. Readers should understand that they are responsible for their own actions and decisions. The author will not be held liable for any losses, damages, or injuries incurred as a result of implementing the information provided. The information provided is for general informational purposes only. It is not intended to be a substitute for professional medical advice, diagnosis or treatment.

This book is formed from the authors personal and professional knowledge as well as lived and shared experiences. The author's aim is to provide an engaging reading experience while maintaining respect for the privacy and dignity of all individuals involved. Where appropriate to protect the identity of people and their connection to the author elements have been changed.

The Readers ideas, knowledge, experiences, and interpretations may not align with those of the authors, this is of course fully respected, your experiences are as true and validated as the authors.

*To my family.*
*Without you all, I would not be me and this book would not be possible.*
*Thank you for sharing your life experiences, allowing me to create your safe space, and supporting me to achieve.*

*To my Mum.*
*For always believing in me, even when I couldn't.*

*To Vicki.*
*(Friend, Editor, Life Coach and LA buddy.)*
*I will always be grateful for that Bonfire Night. This book would not be all it is without you challenging, supporting and encouraging me. Thank you for understanding, for being able to decipher my meaning so the words communicate clearly my intentions, but mostly Thank you for being you.*

*To my Tribe.*
*You know who you are, thank you for the honesty, the belief and the constant support.*

*To Chantelle, Helen, Linsey & Tasha*
*Thank you for your valuable time and suggestions.*
*Your support got me through the final stages.*

# CONTENTS

Title Page
Copyright
Dedication
Foreword
Author's Choice Of Language     1
Introduction     5
Part 1.0 - Laying The Foundations     11
1.1 - Letting Go Of Your Perfect     13
1.2 - Looking After You     30
1.3 – Your Current Space.     44
Part 2.0 – Creating Your Safe Space     59
2.1 - The Bricks And Mortar Of Your Home – Structure.     63
2.2 - The Large Furniture Within Your Home – Routines     79
2.3 - The Objects Within Your Home – Visuals     91
2.4 - The Utilities That Flow – Transitions     107
2.5 - Be WISE     120
Part 3.0 - Strengthening Your Safe Space     123

| | |
|---|---|
| 3.1 – The Minds Matrix | 126 |
| 3.2 – From Chaos To Calm | 138 |
| 3.3 – Your Voice Counts | 159 |
| 3.4 - Be WISE And THRIVE | 178 |
| Final Thoughts | 183 |
| About the Author | 185 |

# FOREWORD

## By Helen Daniel

As a neurodivergent author, advocate, and parent, I am always thrilled to meet others who are passionate about making a positive impact on the lives of neurodivergent families. When I met Jo, I instantly knew I had found a kindred spirit. Jo's commitment to improving the lives of neurodivergent families shines through. She dedicates her time to working with families in their homes and in her community. Her knowledge and experience resonate throughout this book, making it an invaluable resource for anyone seeking to support neurodivergent 'ways of being.'

Many neurodivergent children do well when consistent routines and structures are established. Jo shows how this can be done collaboratively through mutual respect for everyone in the family. She is clear that predictability is essential to calm the chaos that can ensue without this cornerstone. Jo is also careful in explaining that strategies should be tailored to your own family and that supporting a neurodivergent family is an ever-changing and dynamic endeavour.

Parenting a neurodivergent child often feels like navigating uncharted waters, as the conventional rules of parenting rarely apply. With warmth and empathy, Jo invites the reader to sit with her, sharing a cup of tea as she recounts personal stories and practical strategies. She understands the struggle of feeling disconnected from mainstream advice and offers a reassuring presence for those times when you need to lean into what your child truly needs. Her lived experience translates into practical, actionable steps for creating a harmonious household, providing a guiding hand to families who are often left without a clear path.

Jo does not shy away from discussing the stigma and challenges that come with advocating for neurodivergent adjustments. She recognises how difficult it can be to explain your choices to others, such as declining a birthday party invitation for your child. In these moments, Jo equips you with practical scripts and phrases, allowing you to stand firm without the need for exhaustive explanations. Her approach is empowering, helping you navigate social expectations while staying true to what is best for your family.

Beyond these immediate challenges, Jo also addresses the broader issues of parental and social isolation. She provides strategies for building joy into your daily life and advocates for finding a community that understands and supports your journey. Her book is not just about surviving but thriving—creating a life that works for your entire family.

"Your Safe Space" is a heartfelt and insightful guide, filled with practical advice and genuine empathy. Jo's authenticity and experience make this book a manual of support and understanding for neurodivergent families. It is a companion that will help you build a life that honours the unique needs and strengths of your family, offering new perspectives and actionable steps toward creating a truly safe space.

# AUTHOR'S CHOICE OF LANGUAGE

A **safe space** is typically thought of as a physical place that provides an environment where people can freely express their views and opinions without judgement or prejudice. Throughout this book I am going to guide you how to create your safe space. A place where your autistic child can thrive because you provide a home environment that fosters predictability and security. A place that is designed to prioritise their needs, comfort and wellbeing. A place your child can truly without judgement be their true autistic self. A place where they will feel supported and safe. A place you will all come to know as your safe space.

The paradigm of **neurodivergence** encompasses a variety of different ways of being including, but not exclusive to, attention/hyperactivity, dyslexia, dyspraxia and autistic. Using the strategies within this book may support these **neurodivergent** profiles and some people may have multiple neurodivergent profiles, however, this book is aimed at families with autistic children, and so I will reference to your autistic child throughout.

The medical language of receiving a diagnosis does not fit with the social model of inclusion. I therefore, prefer the language of **identifying and confirming** a person's neurodivergence to the medical language of a diagnosis. Being **autistic** is a way of being; it encompasses who a person is, how they think, how they process, and how they learn. I prefer the use of an **autistic person/child** not a person with autism as their autistic way of being cannot be separated from them.

When describing the various behaviours presented I will refer to the **nervous system.** The nervous system serves as the master control centre for your body, it oversees and coordinates every bodily function and activity, from instinctive reflexes such as moving fast to avoid danger, to complex processes like feeling emotions and thinking.

When describing a person in a state their nervous system can function, process, and respond as is expected for them within that situation, I will describe this as a **regulated state**.

When the nervous system's ability to function, process, and respond as expected is reduced, I will describe this as an **overwhelming state**.

When a person's nervous system is in a panic and their nervous system's ability to function, process and respond is drastically reduced, I will describe this as a **crisis state**. This state is often expressed as either a meltdown or a shutdown.

I will describe your **family circle** as those people who live sleep and are involved daily within your safe space. Each family circle is unique, and this book takes into consideration all of the different formulas in which a family may be created. I will assume you the reader are the main provider of consistency within the home and other adults involved are co-parenting. It is assumed other people within the home fulfil the role of siblings. It may be you do not have a co-parent within the home in which instance I assume a member of your social circle may fulfil the social and emotional aspects of the co-parenting role with yourself.

I will refer to your **social circle** as those who you often communicate with daily but do not live within your home. Within your social circle, there will be a strong emotional bond, an appreciation of each other's experiences and shared common interests. The people in your social circle have significant roles in your family's life. Your social circle is often formed from extended family people, i.e. grandparents, uncles, as well as close friends and their families. Your social circle's presence and involvement within your home is welcomed.

I will define your **wider circle** as containing those family people and friends that you have shared past times with, those you still hold an emotional bond with and enjoy spending time with when opportunities arise, and those you see less frequently and often have a limited time frame in which you can share their company.

**Acquaintances** are defined as those you are aware of with who you no longer hold an emotional bond. Those with who you have chosen to create distance between, those with who you do not prioritise your free time to include.

# INTRODUCTION

You tentatively open the front door, you never quite know what awaits you on the inside. Is the atmosphere calm, fun filled or are you about to enter World War III? You hope you'll manage a quiet coffee before the chaos starts. You know if a crisis has flared and your child needs you, you won't get to put the shopping away, the food will defrost and the last hour that you've just had alone will have been a waste.

You made sure everyone was settled before you left. You have kept to the time you said you'd be back for, and you've got treats. You silently hope this surprise will be a welcome one. As you enter, you notice all is still calm. You quietly check in with each of them before making your way to the kettle. They haven't moved, barely noticed you've been gone. Swiftly throwing the shopping into the cupboards your excitement builds at the thought you may actually get to read a chapter of your book while all is peaceful. Coffee poured, you stir in the milk and then you hear the footsteps.

"Can we have snack?"

Within seconds there's now three other bodies in the kitchen with you; each and every one wanting your attention. The calm that you walked into melts away faster than an ice cream in a heatwave as you start to unpick the incidents that have happened while you've been gone. Neither child is able to listen to the other's version of events. As one storms out of the room they knock the drink their sibling is pouring. Your co-parent's reaction to the spilt drink does little to calm the storm.

You spend the next three hours between your children, never quite able to get one fully settled before the other is demanding your presence. *Your* presence because no one else can do what you do. You know this will last until bedtime and beyond. You run a mental list of all you had to do today and start to prioritise what can wait till tomorrow, knowing that most tasks have already been passed across from the previous day's list.

No one understands this life that you lead. You feel a deep sense of loneliness that never leaves you rise from the pit of your stomach as you count the hours down wishing you had someone to offload to. Social media is overflowing with families enjoying days out. Your friends' children all meet the expectations society places on them and people constantly tell you what worked for them implying you're not doing well enough. Every piece of advice has been tried with very little success, you still can't do an hour's shopping without it costing you the rest of the day.

Your family needs a different way of living, a way that

allows you to support everyone including yourself. You need a lifestyle that doesn't attempt to change who your child is, but respects who they are.

Well, now you've found it.

Throughout this book you are going to learn how to develop your home so you can have that coffee. You will gain confidence in meeting your child's needs and advocating for them. You will develop strategies and learn how to adapt your home environment so everyone can thrive and the relationship between you will grow stronger as your child is provided with autonomy within the safe and moral boundaries of your home.

How can I be sure you will? Because I was that parent who opened the door never knowing what was happening on the inside. Even though I had spent years working alongside autistic young people in schools advocating for their needs and supporting staff to develop their practice, I was that parent who never got a coffee in peace and felt out of sync when chatting with friends. I was the parent who listened to the professionals because I thought that as mum my knowledge didn't count, I never felt I was ever doing well enough.

But my knowledge does count. Over the last decade, as a family of five, we have recognised and embraced that we are neurodivergent. We are a mix of autistic, attention/hyperactive*, dyslexic, and sensory divergent, with a pervasive drive for autonomy*. We all have needs that must be accounted for within our daily lives. My extensive career gave me clear insight into how to provide practical solutions and how to develop strategies that worked to create a home that met everyone's needs. My lived experience as a mum and wife to autistic people allowed me to use this knowledge and understanding to create a home which I now enter with a smile, knowing that our structure provided stability and held our safe space while I was gone.

This book doesn't start with an explanation of neurodivergence or being autistic because if you're here, you already know. You may have had your child's neurodivergence confirmed with a medical assessment that gave you a diagnosis of autism. You may be on a pathway to getting that confirmation, or you may just innately know your child is not of the neurotypical way of being. Wherever you are on that journey, it's okay. You're reading this book because you want to make changes to your lifestyle for the benefit of everyone. This book will assist you to create a safe space that meets your child's needs and in turn, supports everyone in the home to live more harmoniously.

I'm sure you can appreciate and understand that getting to this place of contentment takes time, it takes effort and it takes consideration of everyone's needs. As the saying goes, 'Rome wasn't built in a day,' neither will your safe space be formed overnight. There will be times of adjustment, there will be attempts that don't work and you may need to start from scratch but there will also be the missing pieces that seem to just click right in. You will be guided not just through the 'why's' and 'when's' of supporting your child, but also the 'how to'. You know your child best. You know their triggers and their joys, with the strategies presented here you will use your knowledge to identify and develop a structure and routines that work for your home.

My heart is warmed when the parents I have supported who are just like you, send a picture of their family playing a board game together or messages that say, 'she kept herself safe in a moment she wouldn't have in the past'. I have journeyed with families as they have learnt these strategies and gradually moved from chaos to calm. These are the moments that inspired this book.

For too long as parents we have listened to the naysayers, the false promises of support and those with no knowledge of our experiences. Parenting isn't about getting it right or wrong, it's about connecting, reflecting, and developing. Now is the time to take back your power as your child's best advocate and create a home in which they can truly be themselves.

Throughout this book you will learn the importance of the 'why', and how understanding this helps you to connect and appreciate your child. You will learn how to care for yourself as well as everyone else, to build a tribe that supports and encourages you and your family to be unique. You will learn how to adapt your home to be sensory friendly, to guide your child through transitions and to use visuals to provide predictability. You will let go of perfect and set boundaries that benefit everyone. You will teach your family to appreciate and understand each other's needs and you will provide the vital structure that helps your family to thrive.

**You ready?**

Grab a coffee and let's go... the changes start here.

# PART 1.0 - LAYING THE FOUNDATIONS

In our crazy, mixed-up world we all crave a cosy corner, a spot where we can just be ourselves without worrying about what others think. A place that's like sunshine for our souls; somewhere we can grow, learn and shine without anyone raining on our parade. A place where we can let our hair down and be real without pretending to be perfect. This special place, known as your 'safe space', isn't just about physical comfort; it's about feeling understood, respected and free to express who you are.

Before you can establish this empowering haven for yourself and your family, it's crucial to lay the foundations and dismantle all the barriers hindering its creation. To achieve this, you must let go of the unrealistic notions of perfection and conformity that you have been trying to achieve. It's essential to shed the weight of societal expectations and personal judgments; vital to realise and embrace the idea that it is perfectly okay to be different, for your family to have unique needs and to approach life in your distinct way. Embracing your family's individuality is the key to unlocking the true potential of your safe space.

I know what you're thinking. 'Ahh another pointless book telling me to take time for myself, do the impossible, spend time away from my family and alone in nature to recharge'. That is not what this book is. Creating your safe space means tending to your own needs alongside those of your family, finding a balance where your needs are accounted for too and finding your tribe - the people who get you and love you for who you are. It's about making sure your home is a nurturing embrace for your child where they can grow and thrive without feeling like they have to conform.

Yes, you're sitting there thinking, 'but if I've never been able to do it before, why would I now?' The answer is, you've never made the changes before that you are about to make. You've never put boundaries in place to protect yourself and your family as you will now, and you've never understood the power of doing life differently. By the end of part one you will understand how you can look after yourself, as well as your family. You will appreciate that this part is here at the beginning, not at the end of the book, because it's not an afterthought. Looking after yourself is extremely important, when the book discusses everyone in your family, that doesn't mean everyone but you, it means everyone *including* you.

# 1.1 - LETTING GO OF YOUR PERFECT

*Perfection is an illusion that can stifle your growth.*

Your expectations for the human life you were creating developed with each milestone of the antenatal period. As your pregnancy bump grew so did your hopes for who your child would be, your dreams of how this new person entering your family would bring smiles, laughter, joy. From the moment they arrived, your world changed.

You had read the baby books, listened to the endless advice given to all new parents by every relative and health professional who came within five feet. You understood how parenting worked; you had watched your siblings, neighbours and friends do it and you were well-practised in babysitting duties. You knew the path that society would lead your child along; go to school for an education, get a job and earn money for food and enjoyment, retire at an age society deemed you had worked long enough.

For the first few years of being a family with an autistic child you may have followed the parenting approaches passed down through generations in your family, or those that were the norm in your social circle. When you started to notice differences within your child, you were made to doubt yourself and encouraged to 'enjoy every moment'. At every attempt to discuss your fears with friends or professionals you were dismissed; encouraged to wait and see if your child 'grew out of it'. You may have been discouraged from seeking identification of your child's autistic way of being.

The people you had surrounded yourself with displayed the life that you too had imagined for your family. These people maybe had comparable careers, similar family values, parallel interests. For those families around you, the addition of children appeared effortless. The children enjoyed following each other around the garden, screaming and laughing, spontaneous outings were handled with ease. You, however, had started to notice the differences in how your family experienced the days out and the birthday parties. Your child preferred to retreat inside to a quieter area as more guests arrived, often never leaving your side. Every outing took meticulous planning to even get you all out the door. Spare clothes and safe foods were a must, just in case your child fell over and could not tolerate the smallest splash of dirt or moisture, or could not eat the food available. It was heart wrenching, to realise that your experiences were not the same as those around you

As you became conscious of these differences maybe you reached out to your social circle, explaining that your child would not eat the food offered, needed a particular teddy to settle or required the safety of the pram for comfort. Their suggestions were always that you should do more and try more. You may have felt that society judged that the reason for these behaviours was a consequence of your parenting style. As you realised no amount of trying was going to change your experiences with your child, you may have begun to leave social occasions early, to withdraw or make excuses not to attend.

Professionals you may have reached out to perhaps were no better, maybe stating that your child, 'doesn't appear autistic', because they are not like the autistic children they had previously met. Perhaps you felt you were talked at by professionals and not truly listened to just given a one size fits all approach. You may have been dismissed, as just 'an anxious parent' or offered the same sleep hygiene advice to address your child's sleep deprivation that had been tried many a night in your home already. Faced with this 'expert' advice you might have written off your innate, personal knowledge and experience for fear of letting your child down if you did not try the professional suggestions.

Society places judgement on parents when they express they are struggling. People assume the displayed behaviours are because the child is allowed to do as they please or that a parent cannot cope with a child. The reality is that your struggle is nothing to do with your amazing child; it is the society around you. The struggle comes from people's narrow-mindedness that prevents them from seeing an alternative way. The struggle comes from the stares cutting in to you as you support your overwhelmed child in the shops. The struggle comes from the battles for a suitable education. The struggle comes from the ongoing appointments to convince professionals to believe you. The struggle comes from being exhausted trying to maintain a standard of living society expects, while raising a child who just wants to be home in their safe space.

Within the initial phase of parenting, you will have formed your own expectations and judgements of how life should be from the society around you. Your child should be able to enjoy large gatherings, you should have an organised house, have your children at numerous after school clubs. Your child should be able to attend the local school, you should spend weekend mornings at various rehearsals and practices. Your weekends should be busy and full of doing. Your child should be able to sit still for a full meal, your child should be able to eat without needing technology in front of them. You should be able to work, maintain the house, friendships and relationships with ease. Most of these 'should's', have filtered down through generational cycles of parenting and cultural judgements developed from a background of professionals and research. Research that may have now been proven to cause more harm than good. Professionals too afraid to step out of their box, who still preach the information they were taught twenty years ago. At some point, you may have analysed that this perfect family lifestyle you had created within your mind is not for the family you have in front of you. Your life isn't following this societal plan and you're realising that trying to keep up to the 'should's' is detrimental to your family's wellbeing. You're acknowledging that society around you creates environments that are over-stimulating and often cause distress to your child's nervous system. You have become aware of a different way of being, an autistic way.

Perhaps you have received confirmation of your child's differences. You may have sat and listened whilst strangers ticked boxes labelling your child as deficit in areas that met a professionally-deemed criteria to receive a medical diagnosis. I am sure you remember that day vividly. Not for the analysis of every word you spoke, but for the validation you felt deep inside that you had correctly advocated to get your child this confirmation of their neurodivergence and that nothing the professionals said or any given label would change who your child is to you. You may have looked at your child in the rear-view mirror on the journey home, the fear of what the future held for you all flowing through the tears on your cheeks. Perhaps you realised life how you imagined was disappearing as fast as the scenery behind you.

You may be unsure of letting your child know of their autistic divergence; consider the possibility that they already know. They may feel they are different to their peers. They may feel they need to try so much harder to do what appears easy to their peers. They may spend all day attempting to be someone they are not. They may feel like the odd one out in the home. They may feel unworthy and inadequate because no one is telling them their way of being is pretty darn awesome.

Life doesn't end when you have a child that's autistic; your autistic child teaches you a different way to live. But to see this way for all the glory that it is, you will first have to let go of the expectations, the disappointment and the hurtful judgements. The truth is, identifying your child's autistic neurodivergence opens a new level of understanding; it creates a doorway to new knowledge and skills, it allows you to follow an organic path on which you and your child grow and develop together.

You are not who you were before children. No longer do you have impromptu freedom, the weight of responsibility slows you down. I doubt you are the parent you thought you would be, you are not meeting the societal expectations or even your own, so it's time to find the new 'you'. The 'you' who sees their child as a unique individual person, the 'you' who focuses on what their child can do and not the skills they have not yet mastered. If your mindset can focus on your child's present skills and needs, then the challenge becomes one of changing the environment to assist your child to develop and thrive, not one of changing your child. This parenting malarky is damn hard, you are responsible for this living breathing human in front of you. Parenting is not about getting things right or wrong for them, it's about connecting with your child, reflecting on your past decisions, and developing knowledge to do your best in that moment, and just as you think you've got it sussed, you will have to adapt and change as your child develops. To become this new parental version of you - the 'should's' need to be dissolved, boundaries need to be placed and you must become the parent your child needs you to be. The parent you want to be.

From the moment you wake, your nervous system is often in a vigilant state. The intensity of your child's requirements, the ongoing need to prevent overwhelm for your child, means you are constantly pre-empting actions and anticipating what may happen. This places a strain on you as a parent that often goes unacknowledged. Now is the time for you to acknowledge this strain. As a parent of an autistic child, the realistic expectations of what you can manage are a far cry from the societal path laid down for you. Your physical, mental and emotional nervous system often works in constant overtime to accommodate the ongoing fluctuating needs of everyone within your home. Your home requires more energy, more thought, more regulation than most homes. You are most likely attempting to juggle the needs of many people and ensuring your parenting suits everyone's needs. You are a carer now and being a carer places so many unseen demands on you.

Now is your time to reflect on what you do because that's how it's always been done, because that's what your social circle expects, or because it's a personal value you hold. Without accepting that it's time for these societal expectations, the generational pressure and the self-criticism to stop, it will be difficult to secure an environment in which you can all thrive. You are not other people. Your experiences are not theirs and theirs are not yours. Without acknowledging and validating your experiences you cannot change this feeling of unfairness. It's okay to take time, to reflect on the expectations you had, to grieve for the moments you may never have. If you continue to live with this unrealistic pressure of an unattainable life it can lead to parental burnout. It is time to let go of the birthday parties with the whole class from school, posed pictures for your benefit, people turning up unannounced at your front door. It's time to let go of the free-for-all summer BBQ's and friends unexpectedly staying for dinner. Let go of the demons you hold inside regarding your child. Acknowledge the power in knowing their neurodivergence. Let go of the roles you think you need to play, allow others to step into those shoes. Outsource what you can, recoup your time. What matters now for your family is how they need life to be. It may be birthdays split between a few small gatherings, no chorus of happy birthday, no expectations for how they will react or celebrate. Your family needs a structure that is formed around them; one that understands neuro and sensory divergence, that allows for new traditions and ways of doing to be developed, that values and accepts each person as a unique individual. Your family needs you to create and hold their safe space.

You are your child's best advocate to creating a life that supports their unique way of being. As your child has aged you may have already stopped seeking advice from well-meaning others, possibly the advice given held little value within your home. You may have started to adjust your lifestyle already, often not realising the purpose behind the changes. When an item breaks you no longer trawl the shops looking for an identical version, that well-known shopping site has it delivered the next day. Takeaways may have become the new going out, with a side of home cooked chicken nuggets and chips. You no longer shop inside the supermarkets and stroll up and down the aisles planning new meals that would rival the top TV chef, you click & collect the same items weekly so your child can sit in the comfort of the car watching their iPad while you load the shopping. Congratulations, you are letting go and advocating for your child. You are creating environments in which your child can truly be themselves and not putting them into situations that cause distress to their nervous system.

As you become more aware of neurodivergence you may notice traits in your family and social circle that other's laugh off. You may have noticed similarities between yourself and your child, how you both strip off your socks as you enter the house. Take the time to reflect and acknowledge all of the members of your family circle. Are there similarities and autistic traits from others? Have you noticed when serving dinner, you have to make sure peas do not touch the sweetcorn for both of your children? Or perhaps you notice how your co-parent needs to follow the same particular routine on an evening so they can settle. Or is it the friend who journals the detail of every journey they travel? Maybe it's the chameleon cousin, who mimics who they are with that day. It is common for autistic divergences to run in families and for multiple members to be neurodivergent. However, you do need to be prepared that not everyone is ready to hear that you notice their differences. Conversations surrounding neurodivergent traits with those in your circles should be handled with sensitivity to their needs and wishes. Nevertheless establishing who is neurodivergent in your family can be empowering. Imagine being your child and knowing that your way of being is just like your parents or your siblings. No longer would you be the only one in your family who does not follow the societal norm. No longer would you feel the need to mask in your own home. No longer would you feel like the odd one out. Recognising and accepting all your family's neurodivergence allows for everyone's needs to be considered.

When you set out on this parental journey, you had expectations of how parenting would be. You may have dreamed of a co-parent changing nappies, the reality being that they never have. Let go of the expectations you had of what parenting alongside them would be like. Consider your co-parents needs, perhaps they do not change nappies because it causes them sensory distress. Do they often retreat after you've been out socialising? Perhaps they are in shutdown to restore their neurosensory balance.

Consider all your children's needs. Do you spend more time getting one into the bath than the other? Perhaps this is because their neurosensory divergence means they need more support to complete the steps involved. Do you have a child who huffs and turns the TV off as the coffee machine grinds? This may not be because they are missing the sound on the TV, but their sensory divergence makes the grinding feel like it's inside their head. Consider your own needs. Do you avoid standing around in the playground because unexpected conversation throws you off the routine you require? Do you spend as little time as possible in the shops because visually the endless rows of items and the bright lights are too overwhelming? To create a safe space in which the whole family can thrive it is imperative that everyone's needs are acknowledged and supported in a wholesome way by all of the people around you.

Recognising and being able to respond to your family's needs, is sometimes made more difficult by those we surround ourselves with. As you explain why you are making changes for your family, why you need to decline an offer or ask for adjustments, your social and wider circle may have difficulty accepting what you say. There will be people who are annoyed that you now meet your own needs first, they may find it so challenging that they question your abilities and reasons. They may create their own distance because they do not like the changes being made, or they may increase their effort in an attempt to get you to accept their invitations. You may accept the offer without hesitation, grateful that your social circle wants to spend time with your family, all the while internally feeling a sense of doom from the impending impact that time spent together will have on your family's needs and routines after the event.

In these instances, you will find establishing boundaries helps you to meet your family's needs. Boundaries are not about changing the behaviours of other people or convincing them to value something. Boundaries are about protecting you and your family's well-being. Boundaries are like garden fences, they protect your space, minimize harm to you, while establishing and creating distance. Boundaries provide clear, consistent guidance to others that allows you and your family to feel safe and secure. Boundaries can be set with tenderness and consideration while still preserving your intentions.

You may not realise how energy-draining some relationships are until you have established boundaries, but being able to set boundaries is essential to creating your safe space. It may be as you set boundaries people move in and out of your circles. You may realise people you thought held a place in your social circle should really be in the wider circle or maybe even an acquaintance. Likewise, those who are acquaintances or currently in the wider circle may move into your social circle once they are aware of the boundaries you have set. Remember you are making these changes for the benefit of your family. Boundaries are how you will let go of those societal expectations and personal judgements that are holding you from meeting your family's needs. It may feel hard at first to create these boundaries, to say no and take control. It has probably been hardwired into you to prioritise others' needs before your own. Other people cannot be made to honour your choices, but you can show them a gate and a pathway into your life.

As you introduce boundaries and stop seeing those in your social and wider circles with rose tinted glasses of the past, you will see some people are in your life to teach you how to set boundaries; these people may well become acquaintances. When others disagree with your decisions it can trigger your own nervous system. Sit with these feelings, acknowledge past experiences. Are you annoyed at the people involved or at yourself for being treated in that manner? Are you irritated at your expectation of what others should do for you, angered at the unfairness that they don't? You are allowed to feel you deserve more. You are allowed to want better support. You are allowed to want your child to be treated with the same importance, love and respect as others in your circles. Don't fight against these feelings and thoughts, they are real to you. But do not waste energy on battling with the people who create these feelings with their behaviours. Try not to let other people's actions control your life or how you feel. So, they didn't text you back? Put your phone down and focus on enjoying your day. Invest your energy where it is valued, where it has impact on your family and where you are respected.

As you start to place boundaries you may find some people in your social circle feel you are being difficult, expecting too much, becoming overbearing or tenacious. People's interpretations of your behaviours may lead you to question your own and your family's experiences. When those who do not need to advocate and adjust to the extent that you do, brush off your challenges with comments such as, "we've always done it that way," "it's tradition" or "they will be fine", they undermine your very real daily experiences. Setting boundaries in these circumstances can often feel daunting and leave you with a sense of guilt that you are letting your social circle down. Over time you will tolerate these people less and move through these feelings of discomfort, becoming more affirming and confident in placing boundaries as you see the benefits to you and your family.

Society often expects an active social life with lots of face-to-face gatherings, spontaneous activities and as much time spent together as possible. The reality for your family is that your socialising and activities may need to look different. Your activities may need to be adapted and have a more fixed approach. Setting expectations for the activity and ensuring everyone involved knows the end point, is a means of placing a boundary that benefits your family. If you arrange to go bowling, while you can see that in the moment your family wants to be spontaneous and play at the park afterwards, as parents you need to consider your family's needs foremost. If you can see that your child's social battery is draining, you need to stick to the end point of coming home after bowling. Ensuring that you and your co-parent are aware of the end point before starting the activity allows for boundaries to be upheld by all.

Think about the people that surround your family. Do they tell your upset child, "You're okay" or "it's fine"? Do they force societal expectations upon your child, requiring hugs or being able to freely enter your child's own room? Children are often encouraged to ignore their instinctive functions and are shamed for expressing emotions and feelings because they do not present in a way which is meaningful to the person interpreting them. These people are diminishing your child's innate way of being, encouraging masking and not appreciating your child for who they are. Your children need to know that you do not expect them to do things beyond their neurosensory divergence. Your child has the right to be able to express themselves in a way that feels natural to them and to be supported throughout these expressions by people around them who encourage growth and development. You can set boundaries and advocate to those who do not allow your child to express themself freely by saying things like, "Alfie doesn't like to give hugs, he prefers to give a high five." Or if your child is unable to socialise with visitors, "She's having some alone time in her room, we respect that." Once you have shown your child you have their back and will advocate for their needs, continue to consistently stand your ground in the future.

Christmas and other celebratory times of the year are occasions that often enforce traditions on families and may need boundaries to be set. Christmas day is filled with different foods, masses of people, expectations are given to be pleased at the gifts received. Normalise your child having autonomy over the items they would like to receive. Ask your social circle to choose from your child's gift list – explain this reduces surprises for your child and ensures the gift will be well received. You know your child best, advocate for your child if they prefer gifts to be unwrapped or like to open them when alone. If you can discuss their preferences with your child, do so. Explain to your child you want to know so you can ensure the day happens how they would like it to. Do they like to open a gift and explore it or open them all at once, do they want to visit Santa, what food would they like? Prepare your social circle that gifts may need to be staggered and that as a giver they may not get the reaction they expect.

Apply your new boundaries to birthdays and other celebrations. Have birthdays with no cake, bonfire nights with no fireworks. Explain to guests or hosts that you will be providing your child's safe foods, normalise that your child does not need to eat the set food associated with particular celebrations. Let go of traditions that do not sit well with your family; instigate new traditions that fit your family's needs. This might mean that you change a visit to the Christmas panto to a drive around the Christmas lights with a Starbucks. Agree to pyjama days, safe foods, presents opened slowly over the day. Limit visits from or to your social circles, perhaps take the opportunity to go and visit alone and leave the co-parent at home. You can swap these roles depending on who is being visited. There is no shame in separating and doing activities as an individual or one parent with one child and the co-parent with the other child.

Think of past situations where you now wish you had set a boundary. What impact did not setting a boundary have on your family? What stopped you setting one? Often, it's not knowing what to say in the moment, it's an attempt not to hurt other people's feelings, it's wanting your family to participate, it's not wanting the judgement that comes from others.

Asking yourself, 'does it matter?' and searching for the 'why' - often gives the answer to if a boundary is needed. Does it matter if your child wears a coat? No, they may have a sensory divergence and not feel temperature like expected. Does it matter if your child eats sitting away from others? No, if eating near other people makes them uncomfortable. Does it matter if your child texts you instead of coming downstairs to speak to you? No, if it means they express their needs. Does it matter if your child plays his game the entire visit? No, if he's comfortable and content. Can you see how all these answers start with 'no'. You do not owe anyone an explanation and 'No.' is a full sentence. However, if you wished to say no in a gentler way, you can use these sayings in situations you do not feel would benefit your family:

* My child is making their own choice, they are okay to…
* I feel honoured you asked but that's not for us.
* Thank you for thinking of us but we can't commit to that right now.
* I can see my family is tiring so we will be leaving now.
* That sounds fabulous but it does not fit with my family's needs so no, thank you.

However you set the boundary is up to you. What does matter, from this point forward, is that you acknowledge all that you have done for your family so far, the stuff you are proud of and the actions you regret because maybe you didn't know any better. What matters is that you grieve for the old you, but then let that version go. It matters that you appreciate how well you are doing on this never-ending journey; you can only focus on the present and learn for the future. It matters that you acknowledge your child develops at their own pace; that they are unique in their autistic way of being. It matters that you no longer compare them; you focus on their individual progress and strengths. It matters that you acknowledge your family has differing needs, neurosensory divergent needs and that you let go of judgements and place boundaries that support your family.

# 1.2 - LOOKING AFTER YOU

*The greatest gift to your child is your own wellbeing.*

Are you thinking you don't even know who you have become? That you feel you can no longer relate to the version of yourself that you currently are. Never mind - contemplate becoming a favourite version of you.

I get it, I truly do. Perhaps you can't remember the last day you washed your hair, your clothes are bought for comfort not style and treating yourself is a Starbucks while you wait for the car to pass it's MOT. Social media is awash with friends in your social circles having time away from their families, couples exercising together and family days out. While you're grateful that they get to do this, as you hit that little love heart to share your acknowledgement, jealousy sparks within you. For you, a full warm cup of coffee or the chance to shower without little visitors is classed as selfcare. Maybe it has been that long since you did something for you, you are not even sure what you would enjoy anymore, never mind where the time to do something would come from. Maybe before children, you used to enjoy nights at the local pub, playing pool and listening to karaoke or long walks across the moors with the dogs and lazy Sunday afternoons kept your well-being in check. A far cry from the past, 'date nights' are now classed as the rare occasions you and the co-parent make it into bed at the same time and seeing friend's, is a coordinated trip to the park. You don't get spa days and weekends away while your child spends time within the social circle, you get a bar of chocolate to yourself while hiding in the kitchen.

Life as it is takes up every minute you have. You are the parent who is constantly needed, the only one who can support and comfort your child. You're carrying the mental list of what needs to be done, which is overwhelming and exhausting. You are the bearer of the invisible load. You prioritise everyone else's needs at the expense of your own; hoping in some way it will lead to your needs being met. Your normal state of being has become one of overwhelm, you have become accustomed to the weight of the load and you no longer notice the physical or mental strain. You may not be in a crisis state, needing medication and further support for your nervous system to be regulated, but the years of being everyone's saviour, of your nervous system being on high alert, having to overthink, to anticipate and be aware of your surroundings constantly, will be taking its toll on your health and your body will be struggling to return to a regulated state. You know you need to care for yourself so that you will always be available for your family, but doing so is easier said than done.

How do I know this? Because I was the super-organised one; I knew where everyone was and up until what time. I would lay awake at night before doing something out of our routine and mentally work through the what-ifs, figuring out the outcomes for all eventualities. I was prepared for all scenarios when out of the house and took backup items with me just in case. I was known in my social circle as always being in control, I would have things prepared before others had committed. I maintained a super clean house so no one could question our home life and I allowed anyone who wanted to visit us time in our home so I could show I was keeping it all together.

In reality, I was in crisis. These skills were powered by the anxiety increasing within my body as my mental health deteriorated, yet my body became numb to the ongoing ambush it was receiving daily. I didn't realise that forcing a yawn consistently throughout the day was an attempt by my body to make myself more alert and get oxygen into my system. When I attempted to exercise and would feel dizzy, no one told me that the rapid beating in my chest was my heart constantly working harder than it should and that this was a warning to slow down; I just added exercise to my list of ongoing failures. I didn't know the need to prove I was holding it together constantly was unnatural and not a torch I was given to carry upon becoming a parent. Neither I, nor anyone close to me, realised that over the years the anxiety had increased and I'd lost my humour and personality. I was now afraid to make phone calls, scared by the unknown conversation that would follow as the call was answered. Unable to identify or discuss my feelings, I'd impulsively push those close to me further away as this felt a safer option. When the invisible load became just a little too much, those around me who were not supportive of the plans I made for our children felt my wrath. The words from the doctor will forever ring in my head. "I can't take away the family, the support they need can only come from you, but I can take away work". The thought of not going to my sanctuary panicked; me further, work was my saviour, the one place I got to go and be me and switch off from life for a little. I listened to the doctor explain how my body was in a crisis state and how restoring balance to my nervous system would be my only chance of survival. I had to stop. I was signed off from work and given tablets for physical and mental anxiety. Me, a mental health champion in the workplace, signed off unable to deal with the pressures of life around me.

The next six months of my life are the backbone of this chapter. I learnt what looking after myself looked, felt and appeared like for me. For the first ever time I took care of myself. I returned to bed after the school run and binge-watched TV shows I hadn't watched in years. I looked at food and took pleasure in preparing meals to eat and rather than wolfing it down to be available for my family, I took time to enjoy each mouthful. I was still the parent carrying the invisible load, I still completed all the house and parenting tasks as needed, but I maintained the routine and took the extra time for me. Because I was now often in a regulated state I started to recognise when anxiety was increasing, I could identify when my heart rate rose and take actions to slow it back down. I would notice when I started mentally going through the what-ifs, because I had periods where my brain rested. I learnt that I still liked to read and that baths, with bubbles and a cup of tea were still enjoyable. I discovered new things about myself; my taste in music had changed, no longer did I enjoy the pop on the radio, I wanted country or light rock as I danced around the kitchen.

I started to accept the detriment to myself from constantly supporting others. To focus on myself, I had withdrawn from my social circle and the demands that came with them. It was enlightening to see who checked on me; months went by with no contact from those I had consistently provided support to. Whereas past me would jump into action mentally, physically, and emotionally supporting them, knowing the place I was at the reciprocal support was not offered instead their contact reduced. I used my growing energy to focus on myself and started to place boundaries. I removed these people from my social circles. I applied a formula to social demands from those I kept in my circles. I asked myself; do I have the capacity to do this? Do I want to do this? If either response was no, I politely declined. I realised that on the days I only had thirty percent capacity, and I gave that thirty percent to my family and myself, I was giving my all to those who mattered most to me.

Slowly I started to rejoin the outside world a new version of myself. A version I was learning to like. These six months had been the most empowering in finding my favourite version of me. I realised that the feelings of inadequacy, self-blame and doubt regarding my parenting decisions, stemmed from the societal pressures I was moving away from. I accepted that this parental guilt had often made me doubt my actions and respond in ways that further distressed my children. As I learned to trust my intuition, I noticed that I knew what to do; I knew how to support my children and how to respond in a way that didn't trigger them further. The years of maintaining the perfect parent torch had suppressed all of my hunches and shut down my gut feelings. As I started to trust in myself, my children started trusting me too. They were more open to my support and we were able to co-regulate because I was in a regulated state. Moments when my child was in crisis that used to trigger me, no longer did. I was now able to self-regulate and support them. On the occasions when the world had become too much for my child and they needed to scream, I now realised my child was screaming at me because I was their safe person; nowhere else did they feel this comfortable to release their emotions. I accepted the compliment from my child and supported them through their emotional tide the best I could at that moment.

I was enjoying this version of myself; I had learnt that things could wait till tomorrow and that placing boundaries was empowering. I was making sure to keep time for myself each week, even if this was half an hour on the way home from work to just breathe in peace or a bath with a good book. The strangest feeling of all was the one of contentment. My head and my heart felt lighter, I was at peace with myself and what I had achieved within that day.

I don't want you to get to this point of crisis that I was

in before you start to make the changes that matter. Looking after yourself means prioritising your well-being and taking proactive steps to care for and protect your physical, emotional, and mental health. This starts with realising that your energy can be wasted on things that have no benefit to you or spent wisely on things that impact your life and well-being. Like most things in your life, as the parent of an autistic child, you need to do things differently. This includes how you look after yourself, how you engage in activities that promote self-care and self-love because taking care of yourself doesn't mean you first, it means you too. By creating a safe space for your family, you are truly looking after yourself. You are creating a space where everyone's nervous system including your own can settle into a regulated state daily. You are developing a way to a steady life that allows for looking after yourself without adding extra pressure to your load, a way which means your invisible load will decrease because your family feels innately safe and needs less from you.

At its core, looking after yourself is about your nervous system being in a regulated state in which you are in control of your actions and can identify your emotions. It is proactively giving yourself a chance to rest and recover, physically, mentally and emotionally. If we put looking after yourself into the context of a phone battery, looking after you is maintaining your battery, so you have enough power to manage daily life. As humans, we routinely plug in and disconnect as soon as possible. But we don't do that to our phones, we recharge our phones nightly and rarely do we let the battery hit zero. In fact, when it runs low, we give it a quick charge to keep it going until we can plug in to fully recharge. How often do you plug yourself in and fully recover? It's time for this to change. To be able to effectively look after yourself, you need to be able to recognise when things around you, just like apps on the phone left open, are draining your battery too fast, so you can take action to recharge yourself. You therefore have to practise looking after yourself often, so you can recognise when you are regulated and know what state you are aiming to return to. You may need to explore many different means of getting to a regulated state to identify which works best for you and which recharges you the most.

Looking after yourself is recognising that appointments like going to the dentist and doctors are essential to your well-being, are not enjoyable and should not be celebrated as if you've had a trip away. Looking after yourself could be having a nap, listening to music, meditation or a gentle walk while chatting. It might be that you enjoy journaling or feel that messaging your social circle helps you connect with your inner thoughts so you could set fifteen minutes aside each day to message those in your social circle who you are closest to. It may be that changing into fresh comfortable clothes is caring for yourself. As long as you feel pleasure and rested afterwards then this is your version of looking after you. If you are a person who needs movement to feel more regulated, a gym workout or a dance in your living room may leave you feeling refreshed. Sometimes it's as simple as moisturising everywhere after a quick shower or having a different drink and making an effort to eat that counts as your care for the day. You may also find you need to do different things depending on if it is your emotional, mental, or physical state that needs recharging. If you are only just starting to look after yourself, start small and set achievable aims until it feels more natural to you. It can be a walk around the park without children, it may be a bar of chocolate enjoyed in the car before the school pick-up or a cup of tea with someone from your social circle, as long as the time you spend recharges you and doesn't drain you then it counts. Looking after you, needs to be a consistent thought process, it needs to be planned into your days as top-ups and into your weeks and months as full charges.

You have to routinely think about what you can do daily for yourself that charges you up. Can you have an unconventional bath in the middle of the day because in the evening you are needed for the bedtime routine, or could you take the dog for a walk while the children are at school so you can go further and enjoy more time outdoors? Could you spend time decluttering and organising so that your future 'me time' is spent in a soothing environment? It could be that you engage your child with their favourite screen time, get them focused on their interest and take ten minutes to yourself lying on your bed and reading. If your child needs you to stay in the room with them, can you build a Lego set while they play with their cars? Could you start a game on your phone because it is okay for you to have screen time too, scrolling videos or playing games, as long as it brings pleasure and restful feelings. Maybe the sounds of your screen time trigger your child but wearing headphones allows you to watch a TV series of your choosing or lets you listen to an audiobook. Could you hire help or ask your social circle to support you? This could be with outings or with the housework, it could be that somebody comes and sits with your child for thirty minutes while you have some space to look after you. This isn't laziness or bad parenting; this is recouping time. This is looking after you and ensuring you are well and will be there for your family in the future.

Think about activities that you used to enjoy or activities you've always wanted to do. Could you manage half an hour daily to read, build, bake, or learn a new skill? Is there something old you would be held back from doing by societal pressure, could you arrange time out once a month to achieve this, could you learn to ride a motorbike, or finally get someone to show you how to fish?

Looking after yourself doesn't always mean being away from people, as long as when you are around other people their company feels better than being alone. Think about the people around you currently. Ask yourself if you are at peace in their company, if you feel safe alongside them and if their company is as beneficial to your growth as your solitude is.

As someone carrying the invisible load, you may come to have feelings of resentment regarding the lack of any free time that you do not have. You may often feel that your social circle cannot help you and cannot allow you time out to look after yourself. I ask you to challenge why they cannot help. Is this because your child would come to harm or because you feel there would be a more difficult time upon your return? You may feel leaving your child in the care of other people would cause detriment to them and you, but you also need to consider the benefits to your child of having a break from the frustrated and stressed-out version of you. Your child can have time with someone who cares for them and will do good by them, it's not a reflection of your parenting to need time away from your child, they deserve the treats and fun that come with being looked after by somebody else in your social circle. And yes, you can justify to yourself that you need a chance to unwind and come back to them refreshed and recharged. Having somebody else look after your child may take them out of their routine temporarily and you may spend the hours that you return from any outing dealing with a child who's not regulated but by having time to recharge your battery you will have the emotional, mental and physical capacity to support your child effectively. The cornerstone changes you will work on in part two will enable harmony within your home to quickly be re-established.

You will learn that looking after you alongside the family, has benefits and can be achieved. When you feel a sense of stability and satisfaction in your life, you can be more present in the moment with your child, you can feel confident in yourself and your abilities and you will approach life with a new sense of optimism. To nurture yourself you will need to take intentional actions, you will need to think of yourself as often as you do the family and you will need to consider if the people you have around you foster your growth. Those people in your social circle who talked about how hard you have it and how they couldn't do what you do, who urged you to stay positive, they were not boosting your resilience, they were denying your reality, oblivious to how sad and lonely those conversations made you feel. But there are people out there, other parents like you who want to talk openly about the hard moments, who want to laugh with you, who want to cry the happy and sad tears with you; people who can truly relate to the life you now have. It is so important that as parents of an autistic child, you find other parents to connect with. Spending time in the company of other people who understand will most likely bring you joy and fulfilment you may have not yet felt. Everyone needs other supporters in their life who think they are a big deal, where there is no competition between anyone, where no one hates behind the back of others, and nobody bitches about the way one looks after their child. A community where there is no power struggle as to which family is better; one where everyone just brings an energy that says there is no one like you and I enjoy being with you, where there is a mutual connection that expresses 'I'm here for you, I will hold space for you, I like you and I like your family'. These people that you have this connection with will become your tribe.

Having a tribe enhances your social well-being. There is health that comes with having people to connect with who understand what you go through daily. But where do you find these tribe members? You search for them; you search for parent groups in your local area. You start a coffee morning for parents of autistic children, you reach out to the other parents in the playground who stand there awkwardly like you did, hoping the teachers don't come and speak to them at the end of the school day. You reach out to the parents of the children that your child says is just like them. You use social media and join local forums, put up regular posts asking for like-minded people to contact you and let this develop to meeting up with them. You could speak to local community places and ask them to signpost you to local groups in your area. Make yourself available for connection and believe that you will benefit from allowing these people into your space and your circles.

Your tribe will become your group of people who provide endless support, where you feel understood valued and appreciated at all times. They will offer empathy and encouragement that is unavailable from those who do not understand this life you lead. They will support you in your life's ups and downs and encourage you when you feel like you can no longer go on. It is only by finding your tribe you will find others who know how truly tiring it is to act okay and to always be strong, when in reality you are close to the bottom and sinking fast. You will share experiences, memories and milestones with your tribe and you will foster a sense of connection and develop relationships that you didn't realise you needed. Strength doesn't come from forcing smiles and receiving good vibes; it comes from being supported. Supported by people who have that ferocious 'I believe in you' energy, where on the days you feel you can't, they instil the belief that you can.

Your tribe makes you feel welcome as you are. There's no pretending when in their company, you don't feel like you have to perform or mask or get your child to act in a particular way. Your tribe provides support and personal growth. You will belong to a community that understands how diverse your family is, you will find that your tribe embraces everyone's unique qualities and experiences. Some of this tribe may grow to be within your social circle, spending time not just with you but with your family. That is when you know you've truly found where you belong. These people will be the ones who hold your hand when you hit rock bottom and sit with you. They won't force you to take the steps you are not ready to take, they don't give you well-meaning advice that is expected to be followed because it worked for them. They support you as the parent you are, the parent your child needs you to be. Having a tribe will help you to look after yourself. They will uphold your social and emotional balance and you will be able to truly express yourself to those you choose to spend time with.

When you begin to care for yourself and start to find your tribe, you will most likely reach a point of feeling something strange. An unfamiliar realisation that having others to connect with, people you enjoy spending time with, that you and your family can truly be yourself with, has enabled you to be content and become your favourite version of you.

# 1.3 – YOUR CURRENT SPACE.

*The opportunity for growth emerges when you cultivate the right surroundings.*

Now that you understand the importance of boundaries, of letting go of your perfect, and looking after yourself, it's time to reflect on the current space that is provided to your family. You need to look at the impact of the environment that is created around your family and consider if the environment provided is nurturing your child's autistic experience or having an unfavourable impact on them. It is often identified that a child conforms within other settings and then comes home to release the build-up of emotions, but how often is it considered that children are also expected to conform to particular ways of doing within their own home? This isn't to say that you can't have expectations for your family, that you need to allow your child a free for all and this isn't a chapter telling you off for doing it wrong. This is a chapter in which you reflect on how things are asked for and done within your home that could be placing expectations on your child to conform. You have been parenting in the best way you knew how, but now you know your child needs things differently, you need to do things differently.

Helen Daniel[1], a neurodivergent advocate, discusses the autistic experience as being brain and sensory function diverging from the average or expected. She has developed the term 'neurosensory divergence' to explain the autistic way of being as;

> *'a biological, physiological, and/or neurological divergence that alters the sensory information that a person can access, assimilate, and express. By default, autistic people focus on the most useful sensory inputs based on their own individual sensory profile.'*

Helen discusses how neurodivergence relates to differences in a person's brain functioning and sensory divergence relates to sensory abundance and deprivation. (Abundance being when a sense takes in more sensory stimuli than expected and deprivation being when a sense takes in less sensory stimuli than expected) She examines how your child has a different way of interacting and processing the world around them, she defines your child's autistic experience as unique to them and describes how your child's capacity to interact and process will at times fluctuate, depending on various factors, such as anticipation of events, anxiety, and the presence of a spiky profile. Helen talks about your child's needs fluctuating and how they may require lots of support on some occasions and at other times will need very little support in the same area.

A typical neuro-normative curve is often used by professionals as a benchmark to assess the expected development of your child. A normative curve tracks the milestones of children and allows your child to be compared to their peers to identify if there are differences in their development. Society's expectations of what a child 'should be able to do' are often formed from these curves. A spikey profile diverges from this curve, often with unpredictable timing. A spikey profile can be described as certain skills being well-developed while others are still being learnt. For instance, a child may be capable of showering but may struggle with brushing their hair. Aiming to give your child the support as they need it, in the moment, not always in the same way or at the same intensity, helps to meet your child where their ability is at on that day and allows you opportunities to offer them respect and autonomy.

Your child's neurosensory needs cannot be separated. All of their needs, as well as their spikey profile, have to be considered to provide effective support within the home. Each day, your child may require different levels of support depending on factors like nutrition, hydration, rest, exercise, sensory input and emotional regulation. You must also consider factors such as changes in sleep routines, activities from the previous day and variations in how activities and routines are presented. Taking all of these factors into account at any given moment is easier said than done, and not being able to correctly judge their support needs at any given moment can impact your child's nervous system. Having an overwhelmed nervous system is a natural state that everybody moves through at some point. If you view your child's overwhelm and crisis points as them having experienced an overload of environmental or sensory input without them having effective strategies to support their needs, this will help you to understand that this has led to a cascade of emotions. You will be able to see that what your child requires, is understanding and support, not punishments or consequences. By creating a safe space, you are not removing or preventing all episodes of crisis. You cannot stop your child from becoming overwhelmed, not only because the world outside is unpredictable and we are human and make mistakes, but also because your child's neurosensory experience fluctuates. What you are able to provide is an environment in which individual experiences are accounted for and external triggers are reduced, which enables your child to maintain or return to a regulated state faster. This mindset shift enables you to be able to support your child in a way which is more meaningful to them and which allows you to develop a neurosensory-affirming environment.

It is imperative that you find a way to communicate with your child so that they can express their likes, dislikes and experiences. Having the child's voice will help you to understand their unique autistic experience and enable you to be able to meet your child where they are at, not where you expect them to be. Consider being out at an activity your child enjoys. Your child may usually spend an hour at this activity but on this particular day they have a lower emotional and social energy than what is needed for the activity. They are unable to communicate this to you and it appears they are slowly becoming overwhelmed. You can't figure out why they are overwhelmed and they appear to be having fun between the moments of frustration. You are reluctant to leave as this is a change to the routine and so you decide to give it ten more minutes. Very quickly there is a moment that triggers, and your child appears to be in crisis. It is easy to forget how much your child is contending with to be able to process and interact. In moments when they require stability and support to regulate, you can often unwittingly expect more than they can give. When things have been good for so long, you become almost accustomed to this and often complacent to the strategies your child needs you to maintain. In this instance, your child may have benefited from being given a choice to stay and have a rest before continuing or alternatively leaving.

You need to understand your child's autistic experiences and recognise the triggering moments in your home environment that create chaos. Only then will you be able to make the adjustments that count for your family. A trigger for your family might be the bath or shower time. Does your child have a routine Sunday evening bath night before school? Does it work - is your child regulated before, during and afterwards? Or does it add to your child's growing anxiety because they are already feeling the pressure that school is tomorrow and the bath signifies that the weekend is over? Maybe they always have a bath before bed because that's what you did growing up but for your child, being in the water is exciting; it over-stimulates them and brings chaos to the bedtime routine because they are not regulated afterwards. Maybe your child loves the sensory experience of being in the water and the chaos is brought about by trying to get them out and moving on to the next routine within a set time frame.

Perhaps your child wants to wear the same clothes all of the time. Maybe you often end up buying clothes that are never worn because your child needs particular clothing that feels just so. Maybe they have clothes that they wear until they don't fit anymore or are damaged. Is the moment that triggers when you encourage your child to wear different clothes because they need to 'look nice for going out'? Is it your expectation that they will change into sensory uncomfortable clothing that is creating chaos? Perhaps your definition of 'nice' is expecting your child to conform to standards. We often expect more from our children without necessarily realising so. In this instance, the child may be feeling the added pressure of leaving the home and engaging with society and then shortly before setting off they are informed they need to forgo their autonomy of being in their comfortable clothes that provide a sense of familiarity to meet another person's expectations of looking nice.

Does your child avoid certain rooms? Consider if this is when you are cooking particular meals or when you've just sprayed a perfume. Is the smell adding to their overwhelm? Perhaps there are too many people in a family room for them to contend with all the voices at once. Maybe they leave a room when a washing machine is put on, or they may stay in the room and appear to become annoyed. People in your circles may say the child is being disrespectful but maybe they are becoming overwhelmed by the sensory stimuli their body is experiencing. The light from outside is often an unconsidered sensory experience. The sun rises and sets at different times of the day and the brightness within the home is affected by the weather. Artificial lights are predictable and safe. The autonomy to open and close blinds also provides predictability, but do you consider the impact on your child when you open the blinds in the morning? Within the home do people enjoy having sounds playing? They may like this sound to be loud, so they feel immersed in the experience, but for your child, being able to feel the bass or hear the unpredictable laughter may be a factor in their increasing overwhelm. Perhaps you could encourage people to use headphones to control the sounds that they hear.

How many times have you done what you thought was the most insignificant thing, for your child to then quickly be in crisis? Their world ended because you put their drink in the wrong cup. Only this isn't just about the drink being in the wrong cup; it's about the day being full of experiences that naturally added to your child's overwhelm. It's about your child not getting opportunities throughout the day to rest their nervous system back to a regulated state. Many experiences within the home environment could be adding to your child's overwhelm. Often we do not see or account for these and then we have that triggering moment and attempt to fix what we assume was the creator of chaos. We don't realise that the previous experiences have played a part in the accumulation of overwhelm.

We also need to accept responsibility for the part we play in adding to the overwhelm. I have come to realise that when I was frustrated, often because I had lost track of time, my reaction caused chaos for the rest of the family. Irritated with myself that the routines were now behind and that the children hadn't been given the reminders needed, my reaction would inadvertently cause the impact on the family that I was trying to avoid. I knew our children needed a firm routine but I would attend to them ten minutes later than usual and expect them to move faster, to manage with shorter reminders; They would feel the pressure I was putting on them. Our children, as they did every day, had been continuing with their activities until supported by me to transition to the next routine. Yet, when I was frustrated, I allowed my emotions to impact my reaction. This led to our children not feeling supported and safe; They were constantly on edge not knowing which state I would arrive in. My reactions were not providing a predictable environment. By projecting my frustration that I was unable to keep track of time, onto my children, I was then spending a vast amount of time fixing the chaos that followed.

Realising that I had this impact on my children enabled me to be able to make the changes to our environment and to my reactions so that I now provide predictability and feelings of safety. I still become frustrated at my timekeeping, however, I now use strategies to support my timekeeping, assist with regulating my nervous state and consider my presentation to the children at that moment. I take note of my volume and I use a quieter, softer tone of voice that is less triggering to them. I think about my presence in this situation - do I come across as curious or demanding, am I offering choices or dictating to them? You need to consider how you present yourself because your child is highly attuned to your emotions and behaviours, which greatly influences their feelings and perceptions.

Consider how you hold your body. Is your physical presence intimidating to your child? Are your arms folded across your body as you stand towering above them, or do you crouch at their side? If your child is on the floor, perhaps you could get down on the floor with them, mirroring their body. Is your body relaxed and your arms open to enable connection? You can watch for body cues of what your child wants from you - do they shuffle away from you not wanting you in their personal space or do they seek your closeness and creep towards you? Perhaps your child finds it easier if you sit at their side when talking to them, rather than directly facing them. You need to be aware of the impact your presence has on your child so you can adapt and ensure it provides feelings of safety and respect. You will often give your opinion on what could support your child within other environments and how other people need to present themselves to your child, but how often do you consider all of these things within your own home?

I challenge you to think about each room within your home, I want you to think about the triggers that have occurred in that room and how the environment influenced that moment. Be a detective and figure out what happened before the trigger, what did your child require slightly earlier. Perhaps you have a child who becomes distressed in the kitchen in the morning, are you a parent who gets up and puts the washer straight on with the kettle boiling for your morning brew? Does their sibling then come into the room and turn the TV on, is this the trigger? Not necessarily because the TV was put on but because of the presence of lots of differing sounds first thing in a morning. Perhaps your child uses noise reducing headphones when out of the house but when at home they are left in the bag. Maybe the sounds are not thought to be bothering your child as they do not appear too loud to you. Perhaps your child could benefit from using noise reducers in this situation or maybe they require earbuds that reduce the spiky sounds and make the sound waves smoother. You could also consider adjusting your routine so the washing goes on later, or allowing your child to eat in a different room so that the sensory input they receive is lessened.

Perhaps you have a child who constantly seeks movement, jumps on the sofas, bounces down the stairs and drums on the table with their hands. Is the trigger when you are sitting at the table together and they knock over a cup? Does your reaction escalate the situation? Perhaps they could have time before the meal is served, ten minutes on the trampoline or bouncing a ball against a wall to meet that need before asking their body to sit. Maybe they could stand at the table to eat so they can rock and receive the movement sensation they are seeking. Maybe your child seeks finer more defined movements like clicking their fingers, twiddling their hair. Your child could maybe benefit from being offered a fidget or Play-Doh which they can consistently manipulate in their hands.

Think about bedding - is it soft and fluffy, cotton or synthetic? Does your child snuggle into the towel after bath time but kick off their duvet every night? Perhaps they require a blanket, something as soft and tactile as the towel. In the evening do you put the child that's been in shorts all day into long-legged pyjamas because it gets cold at nighttime? Try checking what your child would prefer; your child may not get cold because they have a different sensory experience to you.

To provide a neurosensory-affirming environment you have to respect their autistic experience. You can't dismiss your child's voice, instead, you have to empower your child. Your child needs to know it's okay to say that doesn't feel right, that you respect they may have different sensory feelings to what you do. You need to listen to the child who says they are not cold, who doesn't like to wear coats and who prefers to wear shorts in all weathers, because for this child the sensory experience of wearing another layer may be worse than the experience of not wearing one. You need to accept that your child prefers leggings instead of jeans because they are not as restrictive and move with their body. You need to have an understanding that new clothes have a different smell to clothes that have been washed and worn, that washing and drying them before expecting your child to wear them shows you understand your child's experience.

Maybe bath time is a triggering moment in your house. Have you thought about the changes you could make? Why does the bath have to be before bed? Is there another time that it could be done when your child is comfortable, when your child would have the time to enjoy being in the water when they would have as long as they require until they were ready to get out. Allowing your child choice of when and how to get a bath is giving them autonomy. For your child it may be they come home from school and get a bath, they may get a bath on a Saturday morning or straight after dinner. Finding what works for your child will be a process of trial and error. If your child can communicate their preferences with you always ask for their voice. Sit with your child and explain bath time before bed does not seem to work, offer three choices of when it would work for you, Saturday mornings, after school, or after dinner. If your child offers a different choice, consider if you can accommodate that. By offering choices you are not taking away the expectation or the routine of having a bath, you are explaining when other times are available and you are giving your child a voice in when they have a bath. Having a similar discussion with your child on why they do not like a bath may inform you of concepts you had not realised caused distress to your child.

My child was often unable to get in the bath and when she did it would depend on her capacity on that day. She would have lots of support and be prepared and then she would jump out within minutes. My first instinct was to think the water was too hot or too cold. Upon speaking to her when she was calm, no pressure of a bath that day, I asked her why she got out of the bath so fast. She responded that as she settled into the bath, she would notice sudden movements in the water which triggered her fear of spiders, rooted in once seeing a spider in the bath. It was this that made her jump out of the bath. Together we ran a bath, no pressure to get in, an opportunity to show me the movements. In our bath, we have a shower curtain and when we get a bath this is instinctively folded over the rail at the top, we discovered the water was dripping from the curtain onto her bathwater creating sudden movements. We discussed ways that we could stop this and felt the best way was to remove the shower curtain while she had a bath. We also discussed how I could rinse down the bath just beforehand to ensure no spiders were lurking. These simple changes and respect for her autistic experience allows our child to bathe without distress and her independence skills have developed.

Everyone within your family must understand to the best of their ability that people's capacity fluctuates and what is okay one day does not mean it is the next day. Often when we have multiple children in the family this is one of the hardest factors for people to consider, siblings can easily trigger each other and trying to support each child when they are all overwhelmed is difficult. A child may manage their sibling being involved in a routine one day and the next day they may not. This can be hard for anyone involved to understand. All children must be given the chance to discuss and explain their feelings but also have autonomy over how they need things. For example, perhaps your children usually play together in the living room after dinner but on a particular day one child chooses not to. This child should not be encouraged to go play because that's what normally happens, their feelings should be discussed and validated. This is a great opportunity to discuss with the child who wanted to play, about fluctuating capacities and build new opportunities into routines. Another example could be one child being triggered by other family members watching football. You could support them by stating I can hear your brother shouting at the football, shall we go sit on my bed and watch TV together? This allows the child to know you are aware of the environment and offers a solution away from the trigger.

Balancing needs in the same environment is no easy feat. You often have to go back and revisit why you are expecting or doing things in a particular manner to be able to find a solution. For example, encouraging all your children down to the kitchen in the morning for breakfast at the same time. Why can't they eat in their rooms? Perhaps because you were not allowed to as a youngster. Your children need things differently and if eating in their rooms provides a less sensory overwhelming environment, which element is your priority; that they eat or that they eat in the same room as the family? As adults, we would encourage other adults to reduce their demands when life is becoming a bit too much, but often these demands are still put on our children. When children become adults they can make choices, they can choose to eat safe foods, they can choose to wear safe clothes, to see who they want and be able to work in an environment in which they feel comfortable. Society would argue that these choices are removed from our children as a means of preparing them for adult life. But I tell you, as a parent you do not need to remove these choices; you can advocate for your child. You can provide an environment that meets their needs and you can teach your child to respect their autistic experience. Providing less pressure often opens up more opportunities to succeed. As a family, focus on the achievements; your child ate in their room without being overwhelmed, your child left the house in the snow in shorts but they were regulated. Your social circle may not see the significance or understand these achievements, but to your family and your tribe, they are huge achievements and need to be recognised.

---

[1] Neurosensory Divergence: Autistic Languages: A Roadmap to An Equitable Life For Autistic Children. Daniel Helen, Authors & Co, 10th November 2023

# PART 2.0 – CREATING YOUR SAFE SPACE

No parent can transform their home overnight. Building your safe space takes time and effort from those involved in the family home. Creating a safe space requires patience but it can be done. There will be various adjustments and considerations that need to be made to ensure the safe space is effective, but achieving this safe space ultimately benefits everyone. In the first section of this book you have considered what your current space looks like and the things you want to change. Now I am going to guide you to start making those changes so you can create a home in which your family truly feel they can be themselves, your children can express discomfort and pleasure and you will know how to support them effectively.

There are four fundamental processes to creating a safe space, these will be referred to as cornerstones. When laying foundations for a building all other stones are set in reference to the cornerstones. This same ethos will apply in creating your safe space. Understanding each cornerstone and implementing them will help your family to thrive. Implementing each of the cornerstones alone will have an impact on your home, but together they will form a powerful foundation that will provide stability. The four cornerstones of a safe space are: structure, routines, visuals, and transitions.

**Structure** is like the bricks and mortar of your home. Just as the brick walls around you keep you secure and stabilise the house, having a structure for your family does the same. You need a structure which rarely changes and on the occasion it does, you are required to carefully consider the impact.

**Routines** are like the large furniture within your home. Routines are predictable; just like you expect your bed and bookcase to be in the same place every day, routines provide your family with consistency. Routines can change with the needs of your home, but changes need to be planned carefully to avoid uncertainty.

**Visuals** are like the objects that you use within your home. Your kettle, your phone, your blankets, their use contributes to the experience that you have, they provide convenience, comfort and supports your family's functionality. Visuals may not be essential but having them available provides additional support.

**Transitions** are like the utilities that flow through your home. The predictable water flowing from the taps, the gas heating the boiler. Transitions are rarely thought about but provide essential connections between situations. Transitions can be challenging if they appear unexpectedly.

These cornerstones will serve as pillars of support for your family both physically and emotionally, fostering a reassuring environment where everyone feels at ease and can thrive. Having these four cornerstones throughout your home will create feelings of safety and security by establishing a sense of consistency and reliability. Developing these secure feelings in your children will then enable your social circle to help and give you a break. That isn't to say that when someone steps into your home to support you they would follow each usual step in the day as you do, but that the members of your social circle who step up when you cannot be present have a structure to follow. As the parent who often carries the invisible load, being aware of everyone's needs, adjusting for fluctuations and ensuring routines flow, your time away from the family is often limited. Having these four cornerstones in place that are easily maintained can assist with you not being present.

When I am not present in our home, the co-parent follows our structure and routines as closely as his own needs allow. Not all our visuals are used but the structure provides the stability that allows me to be elsewhere for an evening or occasionally a night away. When the co-parent and I recently had an emergency that required us to be absent from the house for continuous days and long periods of each day, our social circle stepped up and spent time in our home to maintain our cornerstones. We reduced everything we could for all of us to our core structure. We considered the children's needs and the increase in support needed upon our return. We decreased the expectations for learning and installed a weekend structure. We got through this emergency with no major instances of crisis because our social circle was able to uphold the stability provided via the cornerstones.

Spontaneity is rare within our home as we juggle everyone's needs, but occasionally, with planning, our older teen can allow the co-parent and myself out on a date. She maintains the structure, uses visuals and anticipates transitions. Between them the children have developed sibling routines using these cornerstones as their starting blocks.

Building a safe space for autistic individuals often takes more thought, consideration and implementation than that which is needed for a neurotypical safe space. Do not compare what you do to other families around you, even those in your social circle who you are journeying with that also parent an autistic child. You are doing what you need for yourself and your family. It is important to remember this because the steps you are about to work through will look different for your family to other families. That is okay, you need to do 'you'.

# 2.1 - THE BRICKS AND MORTAR OF YOUR HOME – STRUCTURE.

Structure is not child-led or 'seen' by your child. Structure is the ethos by which you parent. I am mindful as we move through this chapter together I refer often to discussions with your co-parent, but I am fully aware not everyone co-parents and so I ask at those points you please consider if you have a member of your social circle who fulfils the social, emotional role a co-parent would provide to you. This may for example be a friend with who you discuss your deep emotions, pleasant thoughts and the rough and tumble of life.

A core structure provides a base for your family members to return to when life in the outside world is overwhelming. Structure provides a framework for daily life that allows consistency to be built through clear expectations and reduced uncertainty. Structure allows for organisation and for responsibilities to be established. Structure is the most basic way of living and is what you revert to on difficult days; the days that you are walking on eggshells because energy is depleted, the days that crisis is hiding around every corner because society has demanded too much energy from your child, the days that you feel like giving in because your mind has not slept, the days that recovery and rest need to be prioritised. Having a core structure in place on those difficult days fosters feelings of security and comfort. The longer your structure is used, the more predictability and reassurance it provides for the family.

The structure will look different for every family as it is built from the principles by which you parent. These principles are developed from your morals and values. Joshua Greene[2], a psychologist and philosopher explores the concept of morality, examining how our moral intuitions are shaped by evolution and how they influence our behaviour. Morals can be described as a person's beliefs and standards that help you to follow the societal code of justice. Acceptance of differences, culture, the general obligation to follow the law or religion and the importance of health, education, and work, are all examples of your belief system. Values are the individual principles that are important to you and affect your behaviour. Generosity, honesty, having respect for yourself and others, boundaries, and self-awareness, are all personal values.

Every person will have differing values and morals so as a family, you need to agree on the principles that will be followed. Some of your morals and values will come from the society you live in, from your cultural expectations. Some will come from the structure you grew up within, others will be formed by yourself or with your co-parent. There may also be principles of your upbringing that you wish to mirror or maybe that you are determined your children will never be subjected to.

It is important that the adults living within the home agree on the structure created. That doesn't mean that everyone values this equally, but that between the adults there has been discussion and compromise and the structure has been agreed by all involved in co-parenting, maybe adults within your social circle who help you fulfil this role. For example, if healthy eating is a part of your structure and while trying to establish this with the children, the co-parent is not involved or openly encourages regular snacking and unhealthy foods, this will weaken your structure.

It is important that when discussing the principles that will create your structure, you consider each other's needs. Plan a time to have this discussion with your co-parent rather than lynching them as they walk through the door from work. Forewarn them you want to discuss creating structure within your home. Agree on a time that is suitable for you both, when you will both be regulated and that distractions such as TV, children and phones are minimal. Discuss that you want to have a debate and that you both may not agree on the other person's principles but that this is ok. Acknowledge you will respect their principles and ask for the same respect back. It may be helpful to set a keyword that ends the discussion immediately and allows for a break. Have a predetermined plan of how you will regather to continue the discussion; will it be later that day, or will it be the following week? If the keyword is used, respect this and do not try to restart the conversation until the next planned discussion.

This discussion is about establishing what your family principles are and developing an agreed structure that you will all work towards for the benefit of your family. Start by explaining the concept of principles and where they are developed. Be curious and show a genuine interest in what values your co-parent feels, thinks and believes in. Allow processing time for yourself and the co-parent to think about these principles and the compromises they and you are willing to make if any are needed.

Explain the purpose of developing a family structure and how establishing your base structure of beliefs will enable you to develop routines and how establishing these four cornerstones together will enable your family to have their needs met, to grow together and to succeed. As you discuss your principles and create your structure, it may help to make a record of what themes you discuss, what your principles are and the agreements you reach. This record can be used for establishing your safe space initially as well as reviewing at a later date, such as when your child reaches different life stages. When creating your structure, keep it simple. Three to five principles will develop your overall structural foundations. When you start these conversations, you may realise you have strong principles but are not utilising them to create your structure. You may not have expressed them to the children or made them transparent in the way family life is organised and carried out.

My co-parent and I often discuss our principles and the reasoning behind them. Our principles and structure have been established for many years now and although they rarely change, I have included an example of when they have. These five principles form the basis of our family's structure, everything our family does ties back to these principles.

The foremost principle in our family is that everyone has the right to be safe. No one should live life anticipating being harmed or hurt, physically, mentally, or emotionally.

Our next principle is the priority of mental health. A personal mental health crisis taught me that I had unknowingly lived with anxiety for years. The learning I did during my recovery, enforces our belief that mental health needs to be prioritised within our home.

Thirdly, we believe in the importance of keeping physically healthy so healthy eating, sufficient rest and sleep are core values in our home. We believe that these provide growth, recovery and overall well-being.

We place value on both academic and practical life-skills. One is not more important than the other. Academic skills and achievements are important and beneficial to us, so are practical skills which foster independence and equip us for life.

Finally, we accept everyone as a unique individual. All of us have the right to choose and express who we are and the way in which we prefer to do things. We respect everyone's right to autonomy.

Taking the example above, our valuing of academic skills and ensuring our children receive an education allows us to build our days around society's school day of 8 am-4 pm. This then provides a weekday structure, as well as opportunities for weekend and holiday structures to be developed. This daily consistency flows into the healthy eating and physical health principles. We have established a structure around eating in which the family eats three meals a day as my child is unaware of her internal bodily sensations and requires us to remind her of the need to eat and drink, as well as for a balanced diet to be encouraged. To maintain the value of the need for sufficient sleep, bedtime within the home is between 10 pm and 6 am due to the structure needed by the working adults and the school timings.

Society has many unwritten rules which we are expected to know how and when to follow. Often the structure within people's home is the same, children 'know' that they are expected to complete daily tasks in a certain order, or they feel thirsty so they drink. In your home, their neurodivergence means that this automatic following of inherently understood rules may not happen. In a neurodivergent house, structure needs to be clearly defined and planned. That isn't to say that each morning you wake and shout out your structure for all to hear, but that the adults within the home are consistently working towards achieving this structure. Having structure forms expectations for everyone in the home to achieve, that is not to say that these expectations will always be met, but they are there to focus the family.

It is not easy to suddenly go from little or no structure to a structured home. It may be that you have a loose structure in place already and after agreeing on your principles you can see where you need to focus on tightening the structure. Some of your structure will be implemented organically over time and through the development of your safe space. For example, our principle of, 'accepting everyone as unique,' is implemented within every action, reaction, and choice we make as a family; it is simply integral to how we live.

Other aspects of your structure will need to be reinforced more directly and this can be done via 'non-negotiable' mantras. Non-negotiables are boundaries that you expect everyone within the home to attempt to maintain, non-negotiables need to be kept to a minimum to have an effect and be easily remembered. Non-negotiable mantras within our house are that we:

* Keep ourselves and others safe.
* Take today, try again tomorrow.

These non-negotiable mantras are used when needed and are often what the children hear and see in our structure. They are implemented through consistent use and adapted to the ability of our children while maintaining the same meaning. For example, when the siblings who play-fight often and appear forceful are asked, 'Are you keeping yourself and others safe?' this encourages them to check in and often creates a pause or stops play. Another instance is when a child was in crisis and throwing books she was told, 'I'm keeping you and me safe by removing the books.' When a child got to the inevitable age of requesting the use of social media, they had the non-negotiable of needing to, 'keep yourself and others safe' written into the agreements we made when allowing them the use of a mobile phone.

Children will need the understanding of 'safe' explaining to them within the context that suits their needs and activities. This can be done via visuals, videos or spoken language depending on your child's abilities. However, it is essential to establish what 'safe' means to your family and role model those boundaries. There are plenty of daily opportunities around us in which these non-negotiables can be modelled. When out walking, as you reach for your child's hand you can say, 'I'm keeping us safe'. When knives are being used in the kitchen and you move them to safety you can speak your actions. Taking the dog for a walk and ensuring he is kept on the lead is an opportunity to explain how you are keeping the dog safe from unleashed dogs. Explaining to your child as they exit the car on the pavement side, this is so they are not near moving cars introduces independent safety awareness.

Repeatedly show your family the importance of self-awareness and demonstrate how to react accordingly, this will teach that ensuring safety is a continuous, everyday practice. Explaining the reasons behind your actions can help your child understand the logic and outcomes, which in turn helps them to process information. My family will often bring my phone to me when it's ringing. There have been occasions when I have declined to answer and then used this opportunity to explain how I am choosing to keep myself and the person calling safe from my emotions right now as I am not emotionally regulated. I will explain that I will respond to that person when I feel able to do so.

Establishing a non-negotiable boundary within your home is setting a clear expectation that is not open to compromise or debate. The impact of this non-negotiable lies in consistency and predictability, it remains firm and unwavering regardless of experiences, ensuring that expectations are understood and respected. The non-negotiability of a boundary serves to protect the well-being of the family. It creates a framework for healthy interaction and establishes a foundation of mutual respect and understanding. If you are made aware the child using social media is making hurtful comments to acquaintances, they are not keeping to the non-negotiable of keeping others safe and so the non-negotiable needs to be enforced by having their social media activity monitored. This is explained to the child that they have not kept others safe and so an adult will support them to do so until they can manage to do this independently. This is your opportunity to revisit the meaning of 'safe' and how to keep safe within this specific context moving forward.

When first beginning to establish your chosen structure and guiding the family to learn and understand the chosen non-negotiables which form your family structure, the reaffirming conversations may need to happen after the mantra has been declared. As the child learns how to navigate within the non-negotiable, they are likely to need the reaffirming conversations less and the conversations will become more focused on further development. An example of this might be the child who had the non-negotiable regarding using social media brings you their phone and explains a friend has shared a hurtful message. You can reinforce that they kept to the, 'keep themselves safe', non-negotiable by discussing this with you and to help them keep themselves safe from further harm, you can help them to structure how they handle this situation.

We use the, 'Take today and try again tomorrow,' non-negotiable mantra on the days when our health is struggling physically, emotionally, or mentally. This mantra reinforces that we can always rest. We can use today to do what is needed for us, and we can do other things tomorrow. It establishes that another day always comes, no matter how hard life feels today. It allows discussions of how our needs fluctuate and what is not possible one day can be achieved another. We have used this mantra when our children have struggled to access clubs or school, when as individuals we have found tasks demanding, when we have had difficult days and self-care is hard. This mantra develops a belief that we can have autonomy over our days and that we can instil boundaries that protect our health, first and foremost.

Having structure in place allowed us to instil a temporary non-negotiable when the country was thrown into lockdown during the Covid-19 pandemic - 'On a school day, we do school'. This allowed new home-schooling routines to be developed around the same school-day structure that the children were used to. Mornings started at the same time as the school day would and were sessions of baking, lessons provided by teachers or clay and similar self-initiated projects with a break time in between. Lunch was followed by large outside play, life skills such as gardening projects, cycling and walks in the countryside. Sessions were made fun, accounted for the children's individual needs and followed the children's interests. Technology – what I refer to as meaning using an iPad, TV or phones used for purposes other than projects or fitness, were kept to break and lunch times. Home school finished at the same time as school would at which time we would revert to the routines we had in place for after school. Providing this structure throughout lockdown assisted with the children's eventual transition back into school. It allowed the children an opportunity to continue to learn academic, practical and life skills while maintaining the cornerstones they required to thrive. Without this structure in place and with the unpredictability of when the lockdown would be ending, our family would have lacked stability and consistency which would have impacted all of our mental, physical and emotional wellbeing.

Once you have a structure, this will enable you to build in your daily routines, your lifestyle and your activities of choice. Your weekends can follow the same structure as the working school week; school can be replaced with morning and afternoon weekend activity sessions. School holidays can also follow this structure although you may want to change timings slightly, for example to give a later start to the day. The aim is that the core structure of the day would follow the same pattern. We use our structure to organise when we spend time with our social circles and engage with society. We build dog walking, shopping, chores, and activities into our structure and develop our days and weeks around the interests of the family at that current time. Our older teen respects our structure and knows that people within the home are settling from 9 pm so when she returns later than this, she keeps noise to a minimum and anticipates that family members may be in bed. When we plan days out, we include a meal at the usual time we would encourage eating in our daily structure. We also plan these days with as little impact on our rising and settling times as possible.

The benefits of having a core structure are most apparent on and after our difficult days. These are the days our children are exhausted from being in society, the days that routines are too demanding and all they want is to cuddle with their familiar teddy and watch the same episode on repeat. The days that we as adults are weary from lack of sleep and difficult projects at work, the days we have socialised and pushed ourselves. These days and the days that follow, we return to our core structure for the benefit of those who need it. We prioritise mental health and well-being, which often means some of our family do not leave the house. They don't engage with society or education. When this happens, we still ask them to get up in the morning and settle at night. We consider personal needs, they may for example require more sleep or support to get to sleep so we adjust for those needs. If they can't manage to dress that day, that's ok. If they need a nap, that's ok too. We encourage self-awareness and respect that their sensory divergence may be more abundant, for example they may need the peace of their bedroom for most of the day, and any interaction with them would be initiated by us going into their space with consent. One of our principles is that we encourage eating three times a day. We respect they may not feel like eating much, so instead of a meal we ask that they just eat something - mince pies and squirty cream for breakfast anyone?

Another thing we do in our home as part of our core structure on or following a difficult day is to encourage physical movement. We allow them to take the day to follow their interest, which can lead to making related items and pacing around the kitchen while discussing their interest. Being self-motivated is the biggest instigator of physical movement. We would include making a snack or cuddling in a different room as physical movement - anything that gets the child's body to change position is movement. Other physical movement may be a game of chase in the garden, a quick walk with the dog or boxing on the Virtual Reality set.

We support rest and recovery on or following a difficult day by reducing demands. We might complete tasks that are normally done by that person if the task cannot wait. We make ourselves available for connection and comfort and ensure we are present when requested as well as allowing the person personal space for rest and recovery. We reduce demands on ourselves as parent carers to allow for the increased support we need to provide; shopping gets delivered online, we outsource tasks which we can and put off what we cannot. Washing that can wait does, we cancel social engagements and delay meetings. We follow the core structure for our well-being during these difficult times. We close our home to visitors and allow only a close social circle, who understand and can support us, to be present during this period.

It is important for our family well-being that we all have our own spaces within the home as a whole and within the family rooms. This helps with our structure of mental health and overall well-being. To make this visual when the children were younger, we used to have blue ribbons tied on the door handles to show personal spaces and green ribbons to show family rooms. Each person has their bedroom which is their space to keep how they wish. We ask that it be kept safe. Everyone in the home is expected to knock and await an invite before entering a person's space. Each person is welcome to invite visitors into the home and their bedroom, however, we do not allow visitors to freely go into bedrooms. Family rooms are used when visitors are present and are available for everyone to use. There is an expectation that if you are in a family room then other people are able to enter. It's essential that everyone has their own space in the home. It is not always possible for it to be their own room but if you can create spaces, perhaps by using furniture to divide rooms, or creating dens, then this can provide a feeling of belonging and autonomy as well as a sense of ownership and comfort.

Using structure in this way allows for further aspects of parenting to be developed. When our child started to use swear words, we were able to quickly develop swearing guidelines that followed our structure – She needed to keep herself and others safe and know times that her swearing may make her unsafe from other people's reactions. We needed to account for her needs as we could see that swearing was often used during times of frustration and her pervasive drive for autonomy would most likely mean that telling her, 'You can't swear,' would encourage more swearing. To address this, swearing guidelines were explained and shown as a visual – written out on paper and displayed. These looked like:

If I swear:
When I drop something
When playing at home
When I am alone
When I am annoyed and alone
This is ok.

If I swear:
At people
At school
At someone else's house
When I am annoyed near people
This may not be ok, and society may give a consequence.

Having defined the guidelines and having them visually displayed allowed the family to all follow the same procedures. It was understood clearly in which instances we allowed swearing and how the burden of a consequence was given by society not us. The consequences were explained as, at school you may get in to bother and miss playtimes, at a friend's house you may be asked to leave. If you swear at people, they may physically respond or they may place a boundary of no longer wanting to be your friend. The consequences are all responses that may be given by society. We found within weeks the use of swear words had decreased. We still have the same visual in use now, and years later when the call came from school telling us that she had been heard swearing in the playground, she understood the consequence of losing her playtime.

The core structure which you plan for your family may look very different to those which I have shared with you from our home. Whatever it looks like, the principle is that, by returning all you do to your agreed core structure, you are consistent in your approach. When you are predictable, your family finds the home unsurprising and with this comes comfort and a feeling of safety. When your safe space feels settled and you feel things work how they should, this is because your core structure is providing stability.

---

[2] Moral Tribes: Emotion, Reason, and the Gap Between Us and Them. Greene Joshua, Penguin Books, October 31, 2014

## 2.2 - THE LARGE FURNITURE WITHIN YOUR HOME – ROUTINES

Routines. That dreaded word professionals throw at you when you have an autistic child. But they do have a point; your child does need routines and you need routines. Most people use routines to help them get through their day, the difference for an autistic child is that routines provide crucial predictability. If you can create consistent routines your child knows what to expect and so this will reduce their overwhelm and increase their ability to be independent. I am sure that you can recognise this, yet you've come to dread the word 'routines' because when you get told your child needs routine, it is often said to you in a manner of blame; your child is struggling because you don't have a routine, your child is overwhelmed because you don't stick to routines. You may have tried implementing routines and found that they don't work for your family, that they haven't made a difference, in fact they have made things worse and overwhelmed your child.

When people tell you that your child needs routine and imply that you need to have the full day set up as this long routine with no changes in to provide predictability, that is not what routines are. What they are referring to is structure and structure is not the same every day. Your structure forms your schedule of activities that you will complete in a day or a week, i.e. rising in the morning and settling in the evening, attending school at 8.45 and finishing at 3.15 with swimming on a Thursday. Despite this constant advice to use routines, what routines are and why they are needed, is not often explained. Rarely will you have been told how to create routines or how to implement routines that work for you and your family, but without this knowledge it is unlikely that you will be able to use routines effectively.

Routines are the usual sequence of events that occur to achieve the completion of an activity. For example the activity may be going to bed, the sequence of events involved would be; getting on to the bed, arranging the blankets, the adult switching the main light off and smaller light on, the adult singing to the child, the child saying goodnight three times, the adult leaving the room, the door being left ajar.

Main routines support the completion of an activity. Mini routines (further sequences of events) may then be developed to support the completion of the main routine. For all routines, the sequence of events must be repeatedly followed in the same way each time. This consistency enables a sense of predictability to develop with the routine and this is what fosters a sense of security, reduces anxiety, and promotes comfort for your child.

Try considering the example of the activity, 'getting ready for the day'. This main routine usually involves getting out of bed, having breakfast, brushing teeth, washing, and getting dressed. Each day you will follow the same sequence of events because it feels familiar and provides predictability while also achieving the activity of getting you ready for the day. This routine can be divided into a series of mini routines. For example, if we consider the element of 'brushing teeth' within the main routine, the mini routine is the sequence of events involved within this element - gathering your toothbrush and toothpaste, placing toothpaste on the toothbrush, putting the toothpaste away, brushing your teeth, rinsing, cleaning the toothbrush and putting the toothbrush away.

Sometimes our normal sequences are not followed or are not able to be followed. The reasons for this can be seen as either a deviation, a change or abandonment. A 'deviation' from this mini routine would be if you picked up the toothpaste and found it had run out and so you had to locate a new tube before being able to continue the sequence of events. A 'change' to this mini routine would be if the toothpaste had already been put on the toothbrush and so an event had been removed from the sequence. An example of 'abandonment' in this routine would be if your phone rang just as you had placed the toothpaste on the toothbrush and you returned after your call to finish brushing your teeth. You may at that time choose to continue from where you had finished or decide to start the sequence of events again. On the occasions when the sequence of events are not followed in order, this can cause unpredictability, a lack of understanding as to what happens next and anxiety surrounding the future routine. The brilliance of understanding structure and routines is that even when you are in a different environment, routines can still be used as they are not place or time-bound, they are measured by the sequence of events. It is important as you go through this chapter that you think about how your child needs their consistent routines.

Some children need routine most of the time, but they can occasionally adapt with support, as long as the routine returns to the usual sequence of events on the next occasion. Other children need a routine that supersedes anything else, without even a slight deviation. Some children need routines which they can easily abandon and restart later. It is vitally important if you are involved in the routine, that no matter how your child needs the routine, you maintain the usual sequence of events so that you are providing the predictability your child requires. If you encourage or create a deviation from a routine, you may be generating uncertainty and this can lead to masking and negativity around that routine or the activity it is part of. Eventually you may realise the child is unable to attend to that routine at all. Any changes to the routine in the moment need to be instigated by your child, this may be them avoiding the usual sequence of events, changing the order or requesting another person to support them. These changes are all okay as long as they are child-led. You would flex with how the child leads the routine, but return at the first opportunity to the usual sequence of events.

While we are establishing that consistent routine is important, it is also essential to recognise that some children like impulsiveness which may trigger you as you may feel you can't deviate from the main or mini routine because you have been told of this importance of consistence. You may also have noted that in the past when you allowed a change then things became erratic. However, in time, when you have a stable structure and firm routines that are used consistently in place, the child will regularly feel secure. This usual feeling of security then enables flexibility if unavoidable changes happen, as they feel comfortable and supported to adapt or deviate knowing on the next occasion, the sequence of events will return to the usual order. If there are occasions when your child does not feel as secure, then you may find they require the routine more strictly. Once your routines are established try to go with your child's flow; the routine and structure will be there to support and guide you.

As adults, it can be difficult to maintain routines; when they are functioning effectively. Daily life encourages us to move at a fast pace. It can be easy to forget to slow down and remember the importance of following the sequence of events. For our children, forgetting an event or rushing through a sequence, inadvertently creates changes that may lead to overwhelm. An example may be if after dinner your child usually has a session of rough and tumble play as part of the settling routine and this is stopped or forgotten about, you may then notice your child seeking this missing event via physical movements or an unusual behaviour within another routine. Your child may become overwhelmed as the evening goes on leading to a point of crisis because their sensory needs and the predictability of the sequence were not met within the earlier routine.

Now that you understand what routines are and the importance of why they need to be functioning and followed, think about the routines you have already within your home. Are these functioning well? If not, what needs to be done so they do? Are you unconsciously stopping at the main routine and not initiating a mini-routine, or perhaps the mini-routine does not follow a consistent sequence of events? Are you expecting your child to be more capable than they can be - have they been taught the skills explicitly for each event within the larger sequence?

Within our home, we have a main routine for getting ready for the day and for getting ready for bed. The events within the main routine are teeth brushed, wash, hair brushed, clothes swapped and clothes in the wash. The routine is structured so the same routine can be followed morning and nighttime. When our children were younger the main and mini routines were structured, initiated and fulfilled by the co-parents. As the children learned a skill within a mini routine, the support they were given was reduced for that event. Co-parents would still be present if needed until the children achieved the full skill set for the whole sequence of events and indicated they did not need us present. Co-parents would then make sure we were available if the child's capacity fluctuated and they needed support. However, by slowly reducing the support provided in line with the increase in the child's skill set we have enabled the children to achieve the independence that they can now complete the main and mini routines often with no support. This strengths-based, support reduction method focuses on your child's strengths and empowers them through skill mastery, self-confidence and autonomy, which all lead to long-term success. The strengths-based support reduction (SSR) method can be used within any routine to develop independence and foster self-confidence, be this shower or bath routines, hair washing, making meals or bedtime routines.

Bedtime is a routine that parents often talk about as being difficult to establish and implement. I want to remind you at this stage, of chapter one – letting go of your perfect. If you don't have a great bedtime routine, are societal expectations, well-meaning advice and personal judgments preventing this routine from happening? Are you of the expectation that at a certain age your child should settle themselves and not need you during the night? Do you become frustrated that after a certain time your evening is being affected by your child being unable to sleep? We have well established that your autistic child has a different way of being and has different needs and that your home needs to do things differently to meet their needs. Please start from this point of understanding before you plan your routines.

Review your bedtime routine. What does your child need? I'm not just referring to what is known as sleep hygiene - a nice bath, a relaxing book and a cuddle. I'm asking about the specific needs unique to your child; what helps to regulate them to a sleepy state and what they need to go to sleep. Do they need to do their bedtime routine and watch TV until they fall asleep? Perhaps they need to bounce around, then have cuddles and then be left in their bed to fall asleep? Or does your child need you to lie with them to get them to sleep? Consider whether you normalise the practice of doing what your child needs – that you provide what support they need to settle to sleep without rushing them and have asked them what they like and what may help. Perhaps you could try asking if they want the light on or off or experiment with different lighting. You could consider offering that they can listen to music, audiobooks or even white noise. Another aspect which you can consider is the blankets that are used and if they need to be changed for a different weight or texture. Does your child not yet have the skill-set needed to settle themselves? If you think about the routine as it is, can you identify (using the SSR method I wrote about previously), where your child needs support still and what support you can put into place?

Routines are not just a means to an end; They can offer consistent opportunities for you and your child to spend time together, a chance to discuss, co-regulate and enjoy each other's presence, as well as develop further skills. It is helpful to have a record of routines and their sequence of events, something that can be reviewed but also allows co-parents and the child, if able to, to discuss what is working at that moment. Giving your child the opportunity to discuss how they feel the routine works is a great chance to for you to learn about their skill-set as well as develop autonomy and for your child to see their voice has value and is important.

The strategies discussed within this chapter can be implemented into all the routines within your house. Family mealtimes where everyone assists with the preparation and clean up can be built with consideration of skill sets and developing routines in which everyone has a sequence of events to complete. Visitors to our house have often commented on how well our family evening meal works. This is because we have a firm structure and everyone has routines to complete. Before dinner is served one child makes cold drinks for everyone, one lays cutlery and one makes hot drinks. The adults cook and prepare sauces. After dinner, the dishes are done, the animals are fed and the worktops are wiped. Having routines in place not only offers opportunities for life-skills to be developed, it enables the family to gather in a structured manner and allows for others in the family to easily pick up routines if someone is not present while maintaining predictability.

Sometimes when you have routines in place, there is a person that is associated with the sequence of events. A change is caused if another person attempts to facilitate the sequence. Sometimes this change is unavoidable but without the change being instigated by the child this can often lead to overwhelm for them. This association can create a rise in emotions between the adults when both co-parents want to be able to assist the child. Viewing the family as a team and respecting all of the routines that need to be completed can help with these feelings. If both co-parents are aware of all of the routines and the tasks needing to be done in the home, then it is easier to delegate between you both that while one is supporting the child's routine the other co-parent could be doing the washing or preparing lunches. Having the family ethic of teamwork and reducing the load for everyone allows for more time to be together and less resentment to grow that one person is carrying the invisible load.

It is like a personal curse knowing that your children function best with structure and a firm routine but feeling incapable of establishing or maintaining these routines. Give yourself grace for all that you do. It is often difficult to remember and maintain everyone's routines, especially in the beginning when they are being implemented. We have established that navigating a neurodivergent household needs to be done differently and that means you may need to draw on strategies that other families don't. Most of us have phones that we have with us constantly. There are a multitude of apps available to support routines, even using your alarm clock and setting reminder alarms is supportive. Think of elements of your family life that need more structure and how you can develop routines and strategies that support you as a family; the more you can reduce the weight of the invisible load the more you can achieve. I have always had a list on the fridge and when I am told a food or household item has run out or running low, I write it on the list. This way I do not need to remember ten items, I just need to remember to check the list. A few years ago I started responding to the family with 'put it on the list'. Now the whole family use the list and we rarely run out. We have had many laughs when magnets have been used to stick the empty item to the list, but they are technically still putting it on the list.

Establishing routines takes time, it takes patience and consistency from everyone involved. There will be occasions when routines become unsettled; you may feel your child is often avoiding or making changes or it may feel like the sequence doesn't flow and that this routine is just no longer working. Before you can figure out how to get the routine functioning again, you have to be WISE and consider the following:

**W** - When did the routine become unsettled? This will then enable you to look at the 'why?'
**I** – Is it the individual, has your child's ability changed?
**S** – Sequence of events. Has the sequence changed from the original order?
**E** – Environment. Has there been some change in the environment in which the routine takes place?

Understanding the WISE will help you to be able to problem-solve how to make the routine functional again. Maybe the routine became unsettled when the usual person involved was suddenly unavailable and the child now needs reassurance that the usual person is not going anywhere. Did the routine become unsettled because of your child's ability? If so, you can consider how to increase or decrease the level of support within the sequence of events. Perhaps you always spread the jam on the toast but now your child is ready to attempt this themselves. Maybe the events have changed order and to get back on track it needs you to go back to the original sequence of events, for example put on T-shirt, pants then socks, not socks before the t-shirt like it has become.

It could be that organically a sibling or co-parent is now in the room during the child carrying out the activity or that the bedroom where the activity takes place is colder in the winter months.

By embracing routines and incorporating the practice of **WISE** (When, Individual, Sequence of events, Environment), you're not just fostering predictability and stability; you're laying the foundation for your family's growth and wellbeing. **WISE** offers a roadmap for navigating life's challenges while honouring each family member's unique needs and strengths. As you integrate these values into your daily life, you're creating a nurturing environment where your family can not only survive but truly thrive.

# 2.3 - THE OBJECTS WITHIN YOUR HOME – VISUALS

As you go about your daily life, lengthy conversations or detailed verbal explanations are not always the most effective ways of giving or receiving information. Often, simpler, subtler methods can communicate more effectively and trigger the required actions. Consider the familiar routine when you enter the kitchen after a long day. Your co-parent holds a cup in their hand, raising it slightly they nod in your direction. You smile and nod back, eagerly anticipating the warm coffee that will soon be in your hands. The visual cue implied the action your co-parent will take. These non verbal routines that bring comfort and reliability, have organically and unintentionally developed over time but you can actually intentionally incorporate these visual cue's in to your home. Using visuals at every opportunity in your home will foster clarity and add to the predictability you are developing in your safe space.

Morning preparations are often a time when us parents struggle to communicate with our children. Think about your mornings. You attempt to use your voice to get your child's attention telling them it is time to get dressed. They are focused on the television and the sound drowns you out. You repeat yourself several times in an attempt to be heard by your child. When they finally realise you are talking to them, your child hears and focuses on the tone of frustration in your voice. Panicked that they have done something to frustrate you, they answer with a short sharp 'What?' Before you know it, you and your child are overwhelmed and heading towards crisis.

Now picture the same scenario but instead of you repeatedly speaking, you hold their uniform in your hands and use the keywords 'Billy' (insert your child's name) and 'Dressed'. These simple keywords will gain their attention and your child will likely glance at you, see the visual of the uniform in your hands and understand it is time to dress. Using this visual and key words puts only a tiny demand to momentarily look away from the TV they are focused on and they can maintain their focus on this as they dress. In this way, you are both able to remain regulated and the necessary activity is achieved. This example illustrates why visuals need to be an integral part of your safe space; visuals provide information in a format that most autistic individuals can process more easily than verbal language alone. It is well-evidenced that the use of visuals helps to support the different styles of learning and sensory divergences our children may have.

The use of visuals should be planned in a way that is consistent. The visual itself and the accompanying key word should remain the same. The keyword language is there to reinforce the meaning, the physical visual remains consistent over time and together they provide reliability in communication, resulting in comfort, reduced anxiety and promoting a sense of stability, regardless of who presents the visual. Just because your child may be able to use verbal communication, does not mean that they can access this method on all occasions, even if they would prefer too.

Let's consider further what counts as a visual and how you can introduce them into your safe space. Visuals are simply any physical cues that aid communication; like the cup and the uniform in the examples above, they are a physical object which conveys concrete information. Anything physical can be used as a visual: your car keys can be used as a visual to symbolise it's time to go in the car, showing your child their bath towel can be a visual that it is time for a bath, showing your child a picture of their grandparents can represent a visit to their house. Visuals can be photos, pictures, written words, text, printed checklists, items.

Visuals which illustrate the child's usual routine and structure can move with you to different environments. Maybe the visual that you give your child for leaving the house is that you put their shoes in front of them. That would also work when at the grandparents or at the play gym, shoes symbolise leaving. It is important that all the adults who use the visuals with the child use the same visuals for the same meaning. If you show your child a bowl to represent breakfast time, and someone else may have to do that occasionally, then this person needs to know this is what the bowl represents.

When developing your use of visuals, it is helpful to consider the structure and routines that you have just worked through. Having a visual version displayed that shows your structure for the day and the week is beneficial to the whole family as it will improve everyone's understanding of what is due to happen. This visual will need to be specifically adapted to your family, maybe you are all at a stage where a written word is suitable and a large family visual with each family member indicated by a separate colour would work. Having this set for weekly activities allows daily check ins of what's happening and when. You could perhaps cross off the activity once they are done. Maybe this is beneficial for the adults in your home but your child needs a daily picture visual that shows the structure scheduled over the day. If your child needs this then I recommend setting the daily schedule as a vertical list, this allows the child to visually work down the list and see when the day is nearly done.

It is unbelievable how many visuals schedules I have seen beautifully set up over the years and then been informed, 'the child does not use/need it'. For a visual to be functioning it has to be used frequently, it has to be used as part of your everyday communication and it has to become a key part of your child's day before they can develop the skills needed to follow the visual schedule independently. Ensure you place the visual schedule in an easily accessible place within your home, somewhere that is easy to get to from every room. Some children find it reassuring to have a look at the day ahead when they rise in the morning. For a visual like this you would return to the visual schedule after each activity to see what is next, you may use the language 'now we, then we...' while pointing at the next activity and the following one. This allows the child to acknowledge the schedule of the day and reduces anxiety regarding what follows. For some children removing the visual and taking it to the activity is helpful, for other children removing it from the chart is enough to symbolise the activity is starting.

Over time as your child becomes reassured via the use of the visual schedule they may develop the skills to check the visual schedule themselves. As the child's skill-set advances, a visual schedule can develop with them; they can move from pictures to written words, to app-based schedules. By using visual schedule supports like this now, you are implementing life-skills to continuously support your child. If the parents in the home see the visuals as a check list of how to support the child and follow the visual order consistently, then this can enable the child to trust the process and allow other adults to support them; thus reducing the pressure on the parents.

The visual described above shows the schedule for the day no more; The activities that will happen for example, getting ready for the day, school, football, bath, dinner, getting ready for bed, TV, bed. To further support your child with the activities on the schedule, you could use visuals for the main routines. For example the getting ready for the day could be visualised as getting out of bed, breakfast, brushing teeth, washing, and getting dressed. These could be on a small separate routine board that can be moved around the rooms with you. These routines could be developed further, if you think of the sequence of events that are followed in the mini routines you could have visuals in the bathroom that show gathering your toothbrush and toothpaste, placing toothpaste on the toothbrush, putting the toothpaste away, brushing your teeth, rinsing, cleaning the toothbrush and putting the toothbrush away. These visuals could remain consistently in the same place. Visuals for the mini routines may be more directly visualised via objects of reference. Rather than verbally listing foods available you can place the cereal boxes and bread loaf on the table to signal to your child they can choose their breakfast.

Using visuals to consistently support your structure and routines develops a sense of familiarity; your child encounters the same visual cues day after day and learns to understand what the visual represents. This predictability fosters security and confidence as your child learns to navigate their environment with ease. Think about your child's skill set and where they are currently at. Are there sections of the routine you only need to be present purely to remind and prompt your child? Could you reduce your child's dependence on you here with the use of visuals? Once the visuals are familiar to the child, you could initiate their use and reduce the prompts for each section of the routine one by one until your child independently follows the visual and completes the full routine. I hope you are starting to see how using visuals can lead to independence and life skills that become concrete and functional for your child.

There is no point putting beautiful visuals all around your home if no one introduces and models the use of the visuals to your child. Consider how you can most effectively engage your child in the use of visuals; perhaps you can use your child's interests to motivate them. If you've got a child who follows a particular football team you could make the visuals in their football colour. Or if you have a child who likes particular characters you can use pictures of the characters to show the sequence of an event. When making your visuals, ensure that underneath each visual there is a keyword that provides the information needed. The key words are not just for your child's use but are also for the adults that will support your child; having a keyword keeps the use of that visual consistent with the same verbal language. For example, the mid-day dinner meal is often interchanged between 'lunch' and 'dinner' in different families or settings, which could cause confusion. If underneath the picture of a dinner plate there is the word 'dinner' then adults are more likely to use that word when conveying the message to the child.

Visuals are also a great tool for using to support choices. For example, if your child struggles to brush their teeth you could have two different toothbrushes and three different toothpastes, making it a game each day to lay them out for your child. Enabling your child to see the visuals of the toothbrushes and toothpastes that they can choose from, reduces the demand they may be feeling to follow the routine and can offer an element of control to your child. If you make lunch boxes for your children to take to school, perhaps you could make a visual that symbolises the five objects that they have in their lunchbox. A fruit, a treat, a main item, crisps, and a yoghurt. Show your child the visual and then show them the actual products which fit in those categories and have them pick one of each to go in their lunchbox. For example, start with the fruit category - Do you want the apple, the banana or the orange? Then move down your visual - Do you want the chocolate bar or the biscuit? Do you want a cheese sandwich or a sausage roll? Having the visual gives the predictability that they will get the same five objects each day, but using the physical items in your house gives them an element of choice from what they can have. It may be your child always chooses the same items, but this is a great way to offer choices and reassurance that the sequence of events (the five objects) will return to their normal if they do deviate. Using a visual like this can then lead to independent skills, your child can follow the visual to gather their items together and 'make' their own lunch. If your child is at the stage where they can gather their own lunch, then perhaps you could consider the next step in enabling their independence, perhaps they could now follow a visual that explains how to make a sandwich working on those next skills with visual support.

Visuals can be brought into every element of the home, and their use is a cornerstone in developing your safe space because they provide so much consistency and support with ease. To illustrate further how you can implement visuals within the structure and routines you have begun to establish in your safe space, we will work through some other examples.

Consider the bath time routine in your home. Depending on where your child's current ability, is at, it might be that you symbolise it is time to get in the bath by showing them their towel, you can make it visual that it's time to get a wash by showing them the sponge. If your child is a little bit more independent but you find that you're constantly having to prompt them - have you washed your hair? Have you washed all the shampoo out? Have you washed your body? - make it visual. A laminated piece of paper can be stuck to tiles or a shower screen. You know your child best; will they need pictures that represent hair being washed or could they use written words? Would creating a checklist in the order of what your child needs to do be able to provide the independence they need rather than your verbal prompts? When creating the visuals, if you child is able to, then get them involved. Allow them to choose the wording and/or the pictures. Think about your child's skill-set and where they need support the most. You can consider if your child knows the skills for each step; does your child understand what rinse means? Do they rinse independently when prompted at the moment or do you do this for them? Ensure you explicitly state each step, 'get in the bath', 'put the soap on the sponge', 'wash all over your body' 'rinse body', 'pull out the plug', 'get out of the bath'. If you build a visual that states 'wash body' and does not state 'rinse body', before getting out of the bath, then your child may, through no fault of their own, get out of the bath with bubbles still on them.

If your child gets lost in time and spends ages in the bath or shower, visual timers are great for showing the concept of time and once their use is built into the routine can eventually be used independently. A 30-minute sand timer which is illustrated on the visual chart as being turned over can consistently be used as a visual reference to move through the sequence of events. As your child's skills develop and they become accustomed to the use of timers the sand timer could be transitioned to a digital timer or a clock.

Some children have the need to know where you, as their safe person, are and what you are doing. Even if you are just in the next room, they may always be seeking the reassurance that you will be back with them. This is another situation in which you can effectively use visuals and provide the reassurance they seek that you will not be gone for a long time. You could use your phone timer to show a countdown of when you will be back with them, or again sand timers will show the concept of passing time. Buying a number of sand timers with a variety of time lengths will be helpful for use in different situations; two minutes, five minutes, ten minutes. Use these timers to visually support the routines you have been establishing. Does your child find it hard to finish their game or come off the technology? Then you could say, 'Here's the 5-minute timer. When the timer finishes, please come off.' When you do this, ensure you put the visual in the child's natural eye sight. If your child is sat playing on the floor then put the timer in front of them and their toys so they can easily glance at it. If your child is watching TV put the timer near the TV so they can glance without losing the focus on the TV. When you first introduce the use of timers you will need to ensure you demonstrate (or model) the way the timers will be used. You can explain to your child, 'The five minutes on the timer has finished, switch the tv off now please'. Following through with this will provide the consistency and predictability of what the child can expect. If one parent allows the timer to be turned over and gives them another five minutes then this is not providing a predictable outcome when the other parent requires the child to stop after the first five minutes. This would be likely to result in the visual being ineffective.

If you start using visuals within your routines and find that they are not having the effect you hoped and not seeming to be helpful, it is likely that there is something within the use of the visuals that is going wrong. You can use the WISE concept which I introduced you to in the 'Routines' section to help you identify where the sequence of events has changed from what was originally planned and has become unpredictable. My advice to you would be to ensure that you and the co-parent or other adults involved with supporting your child, understand the impact of allowing more time before introducing timers, as reinforcing their meaning is harder to do once it has been adapted in the child's favour.

Visually seeing time has a further purpose in the reduction of anxiety as to when an activity on your child's schedule will happen. For example, if you are due to have visitors to your home you can make it visual on the clock by putting blue tack or an arrow to show where the hands will be when the visitors will arrive. You can also do this to reduce the anxiety surrounding when visitors will leave. If your child prefers the digital time, then you could write the time and explain when the digital clock matches what is written, it symbolises the start or finish of an activity.

Presenting time visually can also be used to show how time will be shared between siblings who both need your presence or support, I am going to be with your sister until the clock says 15:30, then I will be with you until 16:00. Being able to visualise time in this way will allow you to explain that both children have half an hour of your undivided time and promote feelings of emotional security. Visuals are often the unspoken language you didn't know you needed. Remember the coloured ribbons on the room doors to demonstrate family rooms and personal space which I mentioned in the 'Structure' chapter? You could take this a step further and have a picture with the door opening, surround by the colour of the ribbon and a picture with the door closed and the child knocking surrounded by the colour of the no entry rooms. At first your child may need both the ribbons and the pictures on each door but as they understand you will be able to reduce to just the ribbons on the door.

Maybe your child is at the stage where they can understand simple concepts like the doors however, they need support for more in-depth expectations. Visual contacts or agreements can be used to support your child in these instances. For example, with a child who is being given a mobile phone, there may be a lot of expectations from the child and you as parents as to the amount of usage time, apps available and conduct while using the phone. Writing a visual agreement with your child, allows what is agreed to be referred back to, but also opens up a discussion of everybody's expectations and allows for structure, like the non-negotiable of keeping yourself and others safe, to be reinforced and incorporated. This is also a chance to pre-empt situations and visually show the outcomes. Agreements offer opportunities to review expectations as skills develop and negotiate new boundaries that will continue to allow growth.

Teaching your children that they can visually communicate with you opens up opportunities for communication that may otherwise be missed. In our house we have found it very useful to allow our children to communicate with us via visuals; this may be showing a pack of playing cards which we know indicates that they want to play, or pointing at their phone when we are near other people which means that I need to check my phone as they will have communicated via text messages. I have had many conversations with my children where one of us is on either side of a closed door texting each other with no spoken communication just written words. I stay close because often when they have discussed the difficult part through text messages, they will physically come to me for comfort. We use visuals in every aspect of our family life; my children will text me pictures of personal items they've run out of and they don't want to put it on the visual weekly shopping list or may write about an interest they would like to explore further.

I use visuals daily to reduce my own load, I use the calendar app on my phone to record activities as events, I record things I need to do as tasks in there and I store birthdays and celebrations with a reminder a few days before to remind me to purchase gifts. I then transfer things to the calendar on my fridge weekly. Having visuals means I only have to remember one thing, I don't need to remember the list of tasks to do, or who needs to be where, or even what I've already achieved, I just need to remember to look at the visual calendar. We go as far as to have a visual menu, each evening meal for the week is written on a list and crossed out once cooked. When I shop, I gather all the ingredients needed for each meal on the list, whoever is cooking within the home knows they can pick a meal that is not crossed out and the ingredients will be available. The front of my fridge is my visual board, everything on there is printed and laminated so I can cross out tasks that are done and reuse the sheets time and time again. All of my cleaning tasks are on a cleaning chart, daily tasks and weekly tasks. This means I know what I have left to do that week and I can easily see the tasks that I do every few weeks to keep on top of the house. As well as helping to reduce your mental load, this allows others in the family to see the load that you carry and opens up opportunities for support. If the co-parents asks me what needs doing after returning from work, I can ask him to look at that day's tasks. He can pick from the tasks I haven't yet done. Him having this choice of task, rather than being directly told, meets his needs so much better.

We have acknowledged the pressure of carrying the invisible load, of knowing where everybody is, what everybody needs and the house tasks to be completed. Now consider how you can make your load visual. On our fridge is another chart with everybody's responsibilities including mine. This not only allows everybody to see the load that I carry, the children's responsibilities, the co-parents responsibilities, it allows for those routines that we have before and after dinner to be followed. It allows others in the family to see what needs doing when somebody is not there, and rather than me having to fill the gaps or directly ask someone I can easily say 'can we share out the co-parents tasks please' and the family members will look at the chart and choose what to do to help. Having your family work together in harmony does take time but is very possible.

We also have a weekly calendar on the fridge, we write on when people will be absent for dinner, upcoming appointments, when we have arranged shopping trips or days out and extra jobs that need to be done. These visuals on our fridge have been in place for so long now our children independently look to see if we are free on particular days and write information on it too. As part of this weekly calendar there is a section for the shopping list, where the family add items as they run low.

To be able to use visuals within your home this effectively, it does mean you need to build new habits, you need to become consistent with writing things down on the weekly calendar, consistent with using visuals as much as possible when you speak and consistent in directing others in the family to do the same. You have to break old ways of doing things and see that in the long run, visuals will benefit you all. It may be you need visual reminders to get into these habits, having a timer on your phone to remind you in the evening at the same time each day to update the weekly visual allows you to clear your mind before the day is over.

Remember, it will take time to build the foundations

of your visual communications. Your child is not instinctively going to know what you are implying when you hold their bath towel in front of them or introduce a timer, however, keep going, they will learn over time and this will reduce the load they carry as the environment around them becomes more consistent. Mobile phones are great for using as visuals. There are a multitude of apps that can be used to support you visually within the home and children often engage with technology more so than a human voice. Small movable whiteboards are also fabulous within the home, you can write out routines or stick pictures onto them and they can be moved around with the person. To create larger schedules and routines you can use laminated paper or composite board, using sticky Velcro is amazing as it allows you to remove and replace the pictures over and over again.

All of these strategies suggested will enable your family to work collaboratively and consistently together. Visuals will become familiar, will bring comfort, ease and predictability. The use of visuals will reduce your load and allow other people to be able to assist in ways you may not yet see as being possible.

# 2.4 - THE UTILITIES THAT FLOW – TRANSITIONS

Life is full of transitions. Some transitions are part of the way in which society divides life-stages, such as changing from a primary to a secondary school. Some transitions come from choices which have been made and then require planning for, like moving house. Other transitions can be sudden and unexpected like those caused by a breakdown in a relationship. We all make large-scale transitions in life from childhood to adulthood, between schools, careers and relationships, but we also experience smaller-scale daily and weekly transitions. In this chapter we will explore these daily and weekly transitions that your child goes through. These transitions, like the water that flows through the taps, are rarely acknowledged and are just assumed to be working - until they don't.

Transitions may be a physical change from one site

to another but it's also important to remember the emotional and psychological element of a transition as this can take longer than a physical change to process. Transitions in the home could be the movement between activities created by your structure, the movement within the routines between the schedule of events or the movement you take when your nervous system changes state. Your child's experience during a transition can be hugely affected by the simplest of actions. If you are not where your child expects you to be, if the support they need is not given at the correct time or if the information provided cannot be processed; This can all have an impact on how your child can manage through that transition.

Consider your child in the morning. They are ready for the day and are watching TV until it's time to set off for school. You finish putting the wash on and notice that you need to set off in the next few minutes, so you ask your child to turn the TV off. As you get their jacket, you can still hear the TV playing. You hurriedly hand them their jacket and turn the TV off. Your child reacts by shouting at you as you didn't pause their show. As you scoot your child towards the door, they remember they need a book and they dash up the stairs. You look at the time and realise that if you don't set off now, you will get stuck in traffic. It takes another few minutes for your child to find the book and come downstairs. When they return you can see they are overwhelmed but the rush to get going wins you over, so you quickly take you both out the door. You realise that as you are late you will have to take your child to the main school reception rather than the usual door directly into the classroom. You know this change will make them anxious.

Now let's consider this same situation if you had used the cornerstones we have been exploring. You can try and plan ahead by going to your child fifteen minutes before the time you need to set off and ask them to pause the TV then explain they have five minutes more, showing this with a visual timer. You could then put the washing on and return as their five-minute timer finishes and ask your child to switch the tv off as the timer was finished. This will allow you to give your child time to process the request and do this with just one gentle reminder because you're in no rush, you know you have ten minutes to spare. You can visually remind your child that school is next on the daily schedule and ask if they need to take anything with them. They can dash upstairs for their book and you can gather their shoes and jacket and meet them at the bottom of the stairs. As they put the shoes on you can put the book in their bag and both of you are able to leave the house regulated with four minutes to spare. Your use of the cornerstones means that you arrive at the school and have time to ask your child if they want to get out the car now and go to the playground or if they would they like a few more minutes in the car first.

Observing and considering how your child transitions at different moments will help you to know how to support them further. Are they spontaneous, do they seem to like impromptu change and are able to quickly move their focus from one activity to another? Or do they take control and try and navigate the transition themselves? Your child may struggle to initiate a transition and you find that they need you to get them from their quiet bedroom and accompany them to come into the busy kitchen. Perhaps some of your biggest moments of chaos in your home are associated with getting your child out of bed in the morning. Have you ever considered that this action is a transition? While some people can wake and within minutes start their day, for other people the neurosensory input received as they wake is overwhelming and they can need time to adjust and adapt to their environment before starting their day. Every child will handle transitions differently due to their individual neurosensory experience. Your child may need you to be with them during some transitions even though they can achieve the activities independently. They may need your verbal support to shift their focus. For some children, experiencing an unexpected transition may overwhelm them.

The awareness that you now have from observing and noticing your child's response to transitions will allow you to consider how you can support them through transitions by allowing a settling period between one activity or place and another, or how you can reduce unexpected transitions. As normal practice my child transitions into the kitchen fifteen minutes before the evening meal is served, this allows her to do her responsibilities before the kitchen gets busy and at a pace that suits her. However, I need to initiate that transition and support her to change her focus. If for any reason this transition is disrupted, she will struggle to go into the kitchen and so we will stop. She will be given the time she needs. We may adapt the routine if she requests this, we honour her needs and adapt the environment then, when she is ready, she will go into the kitchen for her evening meal.

Transitions can often be when your autistic child needs more support and yet they are often forgotten and rushed which can then have an impact on your child's nervous system. Unexpected transitions that your child is not aware of, that they have not planned and for which support is lacking can create feelings of anxiety, nervousness, insecurity or frustration and lead to overwhelm. Difficulties that your child may have with transitions may not necessarily manifest in ways you would anticipate. You may see behaviours that appear to avoid the transition, your child may seek increased rigidity, or your child may become attached to you or the co-parent as they seek security. By allowing more time for transitions within your structure you can provide consistency and comfort as well as showing an acceptance of your child's needs. Giving advanced notice of the changes, reduces the unexpected moment for your child and they learn that you are a reliable source of information. During transitions you can offer sensory supports such as fidgets, comfort items or ear defenders. You can use visuals to support the information you give prior to and during the movements. It is vital that you recognise the impact your understanding of the successful navigation of transitions can have for your child. By providing the necessary support and meeting their needs, you can foster feelings of success while positively impacting their social and emotional well-being and promoting their self-advocacy.

When supporting your child through transitions it is important not to make them feel rushed, I know that is hard when your internal voice may be screaming that you'll be late or this delay will impact on a million other things, but you need to learn to silence it. Channel your inner voice to project a relaxed vibe and convince yourself this is better for all of you. You have more chance of being late by rushing your child than you do if you are relaxed. If you have included transition time into your day and you know your child takes fifteen minutes to transition out of the house, give yourself an extra five minutes next time. Create a situation where there will be no lateness, no rushing and you will both feel the difference.

The support of autonomy (your child's right to express their independent choices in support of their needs) is essential during transitions. Not only does this allow you a chance to really understand your child's autistic experience, but it also fosters feelings of control within your child, building their confidence and self-esteem. Autonomy can be supported by the effective use of questions during transitions. Some children like open-ended choices and directions like, 'Do you need to take anything with you?' Other children like more direct choices such as, 'Would you like to take your headphones with you? Utilizing phrases expressed in the third person can de-personalise reasons you are giving when explaining that a transition needs to take place and takes the emphasis away from you being the instigator of the transition. This reduces the demand and often allows the direction to be accepted easier. For example, 'We can't stay here, the play gym manager needs to go home'. With my children, I have found that the more humour I add into our transitions, the easier it is for them to accept. If your child's vibe is to run upstairs barking like a dog, then join in! Make transitions fun, make it a race - who can get to the bathroom first? Or challenge them - 'I reckon it's a thousand steps to the car, how many do you think it is?'

When you consider each of your child's transitions, assist them to communicate their needs and choices. Maybe they struggle to rise in the morning and you have noticed they flinch at the bright light coming through the curtains. Initiate a conversation with them about their curtains. Visuals can be super helpful for this, you could show them what different types of blinds and curtains look like. You could show them different lights and their effects, maybe they would prefer LED dimming lights or soft mood lighting. Sunrise clocks are fabulous for setting predictable changing light within the room. Trying out different strategies can help your child to know you value their voice, and that they can explain to and explore with you the support they need.

It is crucial to keep transitions in mind when you're leaving to go out but also while you are out and about. Before heading out and starting your child's transition, make sure that you are all set – pack drinks and snacks and ensure your gadgets are fully charged. You need to be ready so that you are able to set straight off when the child is ready, not be chasing around yourself for items. When leaving a place like the park, think ahead about how you will smoothly transition to the next step, especially if your child finds it tough. You might like to plan a fun game for them to focus on or start a discussion around one of their interests to make the transition easier.

It is possible to streamline your outings to minimise the

transitions for your child. If you need to nip in to the shop can you do it on the way home and one adult stay in the car with your child so that your child does not need to get in and out of the car? Just remember to communicate to your child this will be happening so the reduced transition is not unexpected to them. When organising outings solo or with others from your family and social circles, think about how to make transitions within the plan as smooth as possible for your child. Using visuals can help prepare your child and allow them to anticipate what's coming next. Consider laying out a clear plan starting with; we leave at 10:00 AM in two cars, our family in car one and our social circle in car two. You can walk into the cinema with your friend. After the film has finished, we will head to McDonald's in the same cars, after McDonalds we will return to our house and our social circle will go to their house. Share your plan with your social circle, so they know the expectations you have. Anticipate that your child may be overwhelmed after the activity and will need the reliability of being in your car, being driven by you and not having to worry if there will be any unexpected twists. We have learnt over the years that car sharing is not for us. Our children will often use the car as a space to go and regulate, but they will only do this in our cars. They also prefer the peace after the activity that would not always come in a car share.

Think about the transitional things that you do as you return from outings; how often do you walk into the house, take your shoes off and put the kettle on? Removing your shoes and having that first brew is your transitional routine. What transitional routine do other people in your house use? Our eldest child is working age and when she transitions into the home on an evening, she needs ten minutes of my support in which she can verbally offload to me the events of her day. This helps her to process the things she has dealt with in a busy work environment, ten minutes in which I listen and provide emotional support. After doing this she feels regulated and can continue her evening. If I'm not available directly, she will video call or voice note me because she knows that having this transitional time supports her wellbeing.

Contemplate the transitional time that your child needs when re-entering the house. This is often a huge triggering moment for families. Your child will have expectations of what they can do, of what they would like to do and they will often also need time to regulate and decompress from the overwhelm created by the demands of being out of the home socialising. Allow your child to go and engage in their interests, provide a snack and a drink to support their physical wellbeing. It is helpful to use visuals to support your communication and reduce the amount of verbal input given to your child. If your child has just returned from a busy day at school, they are likely to be overstimulated and needing the reliability of their safe space. Upon entering the house are you asking them to empty their bag, get changed and get on with their homework? This will be adding to the demands and expectations which they have felt all day. Consider if the things you are asking your child to do can wait. Could you give them time to transition into the house before placing those demands on them? Perhaps you could allow them time to sit in a quiet room and read or to enjoy half an hour with their favourite game. Perhaps you could benefit from using this time yourself to transition from your busy day to a calmer vibe, maybe you have opportunity to have a coffee in peace before your child is regulated and wanting to interact with you.

When we return to our home, I remind our children before they leave the car that they can have half an hour down-time and then I state which part of our established routine we will start off at. This helps us with our transition. For example, if we return after being out for an evening meal, they always get half hour down time before we then do our nightly routine which takes approximately an hour. We know our children need this down time and we know we need an hour to do the nightly routine and so we account for this extra half hour down time when we decide our plans.

You will also find it helpful to think about transitions during school holiday breaks. During holidays routines often relax, the structure changes, transitions are completed at a slower pace then suddenly, it's back to school. The first few weeks of term are the hardest for everyone as the old structure and routines are reimplemented, while the children are also now receiving the daily overwhelm that hasn't occurred during the break. How can you support that transition back to school to be more successful? During the holidays, if you can keep the structure in place where possible this can reduce transitional time. Maintaining routines around that structure, using visuals and considering the daily transitions will all help to provide your child with reliability and security. In the week before they return to school you can tighten up on the structure or routines that have slightly changed. For example, making sure bedtime returns to the school bedtime can mean the child's body clock is back into routine before having to attend school, this also applies to helping your child rise in the morning at the time required for school. Having your child's uniform out on view as a visual that school routines will be returning soon, can help some children. If your child will be wearing a new uniform, consider a planned transition into the feel of the uniform, it may be necessary to wash the new items of uniform beforehand so it is familiar to your child. Perhaps they may need to wear the shoes or cardigan around the house, so it becomes theirs. If you have had lots of downtime during the break it is a good idea to slowly implement some physical or mentally engaging activities within the last week within the structure of the school days; This can also assist with preparing your child for the return.

Having visitors in your safe space also creates transitions. It is important to consider how your child feels about engaging with people who come into the home. Ensuring there is not an expectation for your child to come and say hello immediately upon someone's arrival allows for your child to transition at their pace. If we have visitors to our home, we let our child know that there are visitors coming and allow them to decide if and when they want to engage. Giving your child control in these situations can help them feel more comfortable and empowered. Your child may make the choice to engage with people, such as having a friend over, however, it's helpful to think about the transitions involved for your child even though they have asked for this to happen. Transitions would include when the friend enters their space, when they leave, and how activities change while the friend is there. You can support these transitions by providing structure and clarity for your child. For example, you could arrange for the friend to come over for a specific activity or set a time for when they will leave. This way, your child knows what to expect and can plan accordingly. Additionally, it's important to plan for the transition when the friend leaves. You can offer your child some time alone afterwards or with you, perhaps suggesting you do something together which you know helps them to regulate. Having this structure in place also helps you to plan to be available for them. Overall, by being mindful of your child's preferences and providing support during transitions, you can help make social interactions more positive and manageable for them.

Social interactions and movements within the home are not the only transitions where you will need to plan for supporting your child. You will also need to consider transitions happening when there are changes in care arrangements, such as when you need to leave the home for a while. Just like with other transitions, providing structure and reassurance is key. Before leaving, it's helpful to communicate with your child about the upcoming change. Let them know when you will be leaving, who will be with them and for how long. This helps your child understand what to expect and reduces any anxiety they may have about the separation. During the transition, it's important to reassure your child that you'll be back and that they will be well taken care of by the co-parent. You can also offer comfort items, such as a favourite toy or blanket, to help them feel more secure during your absence. After you leave, check in with your child, if possible, to see how they're doing and offer words of encouragement. I always ensure my children know they can connect with me while I'm out, this reassures them I am available but often they do not need to connect. When you return, take some time to reconnect with your child and genuinely engage and listen to what they discuss from your absence. My children often give a narrative of what has happened and even though I may be aware of their activities, I listen to each child's voice and their feelings and opinion; this helps to reinforce a sense of security and trust in my relationship with them. By being mindful of your child's emotions and needs during transitions, whether it's social interactions, changes in care arrangements, or movements within the home you can provide the support and reassurance they need to navigate these changes smoothly.

# 2.5 - BE WISE

Within the chapters that form Part two,' Creating your safe space', you have learned about the importance of structure, routines, visuals and transitions. Implementing all of these cornerstones into your home will establish a safe space for your family to develop and thrive. This does not mean that you won't have times where you feel that these cornerstones you have put in place are messed up and are going completely wrong no matter what you seem to do. When this happens it is so easy to think that the cornerstones do not help your family or that having the cornerstones in place is not worth it, however, it is always worth the short-term kickback you may initially receive from your child or the family to reinstate the cornerstones. Having these cornerstones in place will enable your family to feel supported and understood; you will be fostering positive relationships and enabling communication between you all. These cornerstones will support your family to thrive long-term.

During the chapter, Routines, you learnt about the **WISE** approach. **WISE** stands for the **W**hen, the Individual, the **S**equence of events, and the **E**nvironment. The **WISE** approach can be applied to any of the cornerstones to help you figure out why they are not working in an efficient manner and what needs to be done to get them functional again. Below are some examples of how **WISE** can be used to review and reinstate the functionality of the cornerstones.

Maybe you feel that your structure has become unsettled. You look at **W**hen and realise this has been after you had a weekend away, your rise and settle structure changed and needs to be brought back to fit in with the working school week. Or it may be that an **I**ndividual's ability to maintain the structure has changed, perhaps the co-parent is under stress at work which is impacting their ability to stick to the non-negotiables and during this period you need to support them to do so. It could be the **S**equence of events that has changed within your structure. The co-parent's working hours may have altered meaning they now return home midafternoon not later in the day as expected. Has the **E**nvironment changed - maybe the clocks go back and so it is lighter and darker at differing times.

Perhaps the use of visuals has become unsettled, looking at **W**hen, you realise this was after the summer break and because visuals that apply to school routines had not been used during that time your child is unsettled when you reintroduce them. It could be your child's **I**ndividual skills have developed past the current pictures being used. Asking your child to update the visuals with you provides you with their voice and you find they now feel they want to use written words rather than pictures. It could be the **S**equence of events has changed which you allowed because it seemed to be working but a few weeks in, it's actually causing distress. Or has the **E**nvironment changed - perhaps a timer got broken and you have been using the phone timer instead of a sand timer.

It could be that a particular transition is unsettled and each time you offer support the atmosphere becomes fraught. You consider **W**hen and realise during the start of the transition your attention is not given to the child and although physically present you are not supporting them, you are in discussion with the co-parent. It may be that your child's **I**ndividual needs have changed and now they need prompts and not direct support. It could be the **S**equence of events that has changed. Rather than the fifteen minutes you were allowing to transition, because it was going well you have organically reduced this to ten, but now your child feels rushed. Have you changed the **E**nvironment, is their jacket kept in a different place or are they being asked to walk instead of going in the car?

As the cornerstones are firmly established within your home they will foster sustained development and predictability. Applying the **WISE** approach to assess and review your cornerstones will help to create and maintain the secure nurturing atmosphere your family requires.

# PART 3.0 - STRENGTHENING YOUR SAFE SPACE

As a parent to an autistic child you just know. It's a radar your body has developed over the years, an intuitive awareness of your child's needs. Such as at the park, you notice before other parents do that the slide is empty, you innately know your child will be blocking the top, triggered into crisis by the unpredictability of the environment around them. You can see it in your child's eyes when they leave their peer group and make their way to you leaving a trail of destruction in their wake, overwhelmed by the social injustice when the rules of the game have been changed. You know when they walk out of school and the teacher tells you 'They've been fine', that means they have not shown their true state and this evening will be a challenge for you all. As their parent you know they are far from fine, you have become highly tuned into the significance of the little signs as you have invested in getting to know your child.

You may know that your child has times when they appear calm and content happy to just 'be'. Yet perhaps you may feel that most of the time you are walking on a carpet of eggshells, never quite sure what will tip your child over the edge. You desperately try to help your child, you can see they are in crisis but everything you do seems to agitate them further. There's a disconnect between you both, your child is unknowingly seeking for something that you do not know how or when to provide.

Throughout the book so far you have learned how to lay the foundations for a new way of living. You have discovered how to develop four cornerstones within your home environment to support your family to live in harmony and how to 'be **WISE**' when those cornerstones do not appear to be effective. But sometimes even with the steps you have taken so far, there may still be a divide between your child and you that you cannot seem to close, following the steps does not seem enough you want to support your child but nothing seems to help for long. You want to transform your home from one of hesitant tension, walking on eggshells awaiting the inevitable meltdown, to a far more relaxed, generally calm and positive place, but don't seem to be able to.

In part 3, we are going to explore the minds matrix. You are going to unlock the secrets of how our operating systems work and understand the states your child's nervous system goes through. Then you are going to learn how to support your child when in these various states, the importance of time, and honouring their needs. You are going to learn how to restore your child's balance and adapt the environment to suit their needs, then you will be empowered to advocate for your child and when they are ready, teach them how to advocate for themselves.

The aim of this will be that you are going to reconnect with your child, you are going to teach them that you have their back, that you acknowledge and validate their experiences. The relationship you have together will become equal and stronger as your child learns you truly want to help them **THRIVE.**

# 3.1 – THE MINDS MATRIX

*Within the intricacy of the mind's matrix lies the blueprint of our essence.*

Much like Apple's iOS or Android on a phone, you can consider the nervous system to be the operating system of the body. Just as these operating systems manage the functioning of the phone, processing the data and responding to the input given by you, our nervous system manages the functioning of the body. The nervous system is responsible for interpreting the sensory and neurological information the body receives. For example, when you enter a familiar place your nervous system triggers emotions and memories associated with past experiences in that setting. The nervous system is a complex reactive system that continuously processes, responds and controls the body's functions; managing everything from reflexes to thoughts and emotions. It is responsible for ensuring a person's wellbeing and survival. If you were to sip a drink that is too hot, your nervous system would quickly recognise this and respond by sending signals to move your hand and prevent you causing further harm to yourself.

Our bodies nervous system response will differ. What one person perceives as a minor occurrence another may interpret as a substantial challenge. This is because everyone's responses are shaped by their personal neurosensory divergence. Although you and your child may collectively experience the same event, your responses will be inherently unique, influenced by the individual working of your nervous system.

Think about your phone. Each time you ask it to do something, you expect the phone to process, respond and function as requested. Our nervous system should do the same. When our nervous system is in a state at which it can function, process and respond as is expected for a person within that situation, this is known as being 'regulated'. When the nervous system is 'overwhelmed', this ability to function, process and respond is reduced, much like when your phone glitches and randomly closes the application.

When the nervous system's ability to function, process and respond is drastically reduced this can be described as 'crisis'. At this point the nervous system is in a panic state. If your child outwardly displays this crisis with behaviour that appears stubborn, selective or confrontational, this may be referred to as a 'meltdown'. Or, your child may internalise this crisis state which is often described as 'shutting down,' with behaviours that may appear as mutism, sulking, or refusal. Regardless of which presentation your child displays, their nervous system is in crisis - their ability to function is drastically reduced as is their ability to control how their nervous system responds to experiences. This crisis state is like your phone when it has frozen. No matter how much you press those buttons, it cannot respond until the operating system has been restored.

While your child's nervous system is in a state of crisis, their brain is experiencing extreme stress. Telling your child to stop crying, to explain what's happened or trying to guilt them out of the crisis with consequences is futile; your child's nervous system is unable to reason logically. Doing any of these things could be detrimental to your child's wellbeing and further increase the panic your child is experiencing. You may have a child who lashes out when in this state and harms themselves or others. Perhaps your child shouts and screams or runs away. You may have a child who hides physically or a child who retreats inwards and cannot talk or walk. Your child may curl up tightly and sob. However your child presents when their nervous system is in a crisis state, please know it is as exhausting for them as it is for you. The aim, nevertheless, always needs to be ensuring your child feels safe by effectively communicating with them and being compassionate to their experiences. Your child isn't purposefully trying to make things difficult; they're not trying to irritate or provoke you. Your child is not choosing to enter this crisis state; they are struggling and need your support to restore their nervous system to a regulated state.

When a child is in crisis, the first priority is to help your child's nervous system return to a regulated state, no one can think logically, develop or learn if their nervous system is not in a regulated state. Just like you have observed and carefully watched your child, learning the early signs to be able to instinctively know when they are in a crisis or an overwhelmed state, you can learn how they present when their nervous system is regulated. Being regulated varies from person to person in presentation. Often this state is presented in a relaxed, peaceful but joyful manner; your child may swirl around while watching their favourite show, they may line up their toys, play on their PC or sit stroking the dog. You may notice that your child is more able to express their needs and request connection and comfort when they are in their regulated state or for you it may be the state in which you realise at the end of the evening that you are content. You can only guide your child to a regulated state if you know what this looks like for them. Once you have this understanding of their regulated state you can teach your child how a regulated state presents for them. You can discuss what this feels like and what they can do to help maintain this balance or restore it when their nervous system is overwhelmed or in crisis.

It is crucial as their parent that you try to acknowledge and appreciate the states your child's nervous system can be in through no fault of their own. Only with this acceptance can you then truly attempt to support your child to be regulated more often. Be aware however, that even though you may do everything within your power to try and maintain your child being in their regulated state, there may be times this may not suffice and your child will transition from a regulated state to being overwhelmed or in crisis. Remember, this is not a reflection of a lack of effort on your behalf – it is a consequence of the complexities of your child's needs and the environment.

You may have noticed through getting to know your child that you can recognise signs that happen before they are in crisis. This is their body communicating that the nervous system is overwhelmed. Similar to the crisis state, during overwhelm, your child's skills and needs are not the same as when they are regulated. Their ability to respond, process and function is reduced, and this means the skills they have when regulated are now not as accessible to them. When a child is overwhelmed their language skills may reduce, their understanding and communication skills may not appear as they usually do and they may become physically unable to complete tasks.

In this nervous system state your child may present as verbally argumentative; you may feel they are answering back or shouting at you. They may appear easily frustrated and have a lower tolerance to things which they usually accept. They may verbally ramble with no context to their talk or bang objects with little regard to the consequences. They may slam doors shut, sighing, or grunting as they leave the room. Your child could appear to not be listening to what is being spoken to them, seem zoned out or they may move slower than expected. They may leave routines incomplete or appear to have forgotten the simplest of tasks. It is easy for those in your family or social circles to become frustrated when your child is in this overwhelmed state if they lack understanding of your child's overwhelm. Sometimes when a child is overwhelmed it may appear that they are searching for something to go wrong, purposefully creating instances when they can then express this overwhelm. Perhaps your child has returned home in what initially appears as a regulated state and then within minutes begins criticising you or seems to suddenly become overwhelmed from the smallest thing. Maybe you left their book on the table or the cup you gave them was a little wet. It may feel like you can do nothing right for you child, that you are always the last rain drop that sends the water flooding out of the bucket. Consider in these instances that your child may have been containing their feelings of overwhelm all day; it is not you that over- filled their bucket. You are your child's safe, predictable person so now they can let their emotions pour out.

It may be helpful for you to learn how your child presents when overwhelmed and what their triggers are, so you can try to assist them to return to a regulated state and release those emotions without detriment to themselves or others. Be aware though, that sometimes your child may not display their state outwardly and so when they are overwhelmed you may not initially realise until it is too late. Also, the transition from a regulated state to crisis state may happen so fast that there are no warning signs in which you can support the child.

Let's look at the example of an evening meal to understand the different nervous system states more.

Imagine that your whole family are sitting together around the table. One evening your child may join in with the conversations, eat the meal and enjoy watching the show playing on the kitchen TV. Your nervous system responses are regulated, you respond in the same way; you notice you feel contentment with this family activity. You know that the meal you provided was food your child prefers and often eats, the TV show was their choice and they seem to have enjoyed the day's activities. Both you and your child can process, respond and function as is expected for each of you as your nervous system states are regulated.

Another evening, in the same situation, your child may not eat much of their meal, they appear frustrated when you ask a question and you notice they are picking their fingernails. When the characters on the TV laugh, your child bangs their cup on to the table and sighs heavily. Your experience is still that the family is enjoying a nice meal, however, your child is having a different experience- the meal has not been cooked exactly how it usually is, they are worrying about a maths question they could not figure out at school, the volume on the TV is slightly louder than the previous day, meaning when the characters laugh it sounds harsher. Your child's nervous system can no longer process all this input at once. As their nervous system is overwhelmed, their ability to process, function and respond as is expected has been reduced. Their overwhelm is expressed via the banging of the cup and the expelling of air from the body.

On a different evening, the same evening meal situation is altered as your other child has a friend over. This means there is another person at the table and the conversation is louder and more continuous than usual. Your autistic child is about to start eating when the invited friend goes to put ketchup on their food. As the invited child taps the bottom of the bottle, ketchup flies out and lands on your autistic child's food. The other children laugh but your autistic child screams and throws their plate to the floor, leaving the room cursing at the invited friend. Everyone else's experience was relaxed and kept their nervous system regulated, but for your autistic child, the constant conversation was overwhelming, the friend's laugh hurt their ears and they don't like the smell and taste of ketchup. As the ketchup landed on their plate your child's nervous system has panicked and is unable to process all this input. Your child is in crisis as their ability to process, respond and function as expected is drastically reduced. They cannot reason or regulate and their nervous system feels it is being attacked.

Beneath these responses is a child seeking connection, understanding and respect for their autistic experience. Imposing punishments on a child for the behaviours they have displayed in such examples, fails to address the underlying complexities of their needs. Punishment is likely to cause strained relationships and may leave your child with unaddressed feelings of despair. Punishment rather than seeking understanding may also cause your child to develop difficulties in navigating future challenges and relationships or to display behaviours to protect themselves, like masking their true state. The duration and intensity of your child's nervous system response not only impacts them in the present but also influences their future experiences. If your child's autistic experience is dismissed or invalidated, it can contribute to a diminished sense of self-worth and confidence.

When you or others from within your circles are supporting your child during overwhelm or crisis, it is helpful to try and put your own emotions aside; this may feel really hard but even taking a quick internal count backwards from 10 can help you to pause before responding. The crisis and overwhelm states are not the time for teaching, reasoning or explaining. Trying to rush your child to regulate because your own state is overwhelmed, even subtly, has a huge chance of backfiring and will take you longer than taking a moment to regulate yourself and doing it in the way your child needed in the first place. To be able to effectively support your child you need to work on being in the regulated state yourself, take a few moments to deep breathe, see your child as being in a panic state not as having a tantrum. Focus on your child not the environment around you both. I am not saying your child can never see your range of emotions, but they can only learn from positive role modelling once they are in the regulated state and able to process. To guide your child to a regulated state you need to be able to stay close and provide reassurance while meeting your child's needs where they are, not where you expect them to be.

A positive consequence of the predictability and security of the environment you now provide, may be that your child's nervous system is more often in a regulated state. You may then be caught unawares when either your child now navigates an activity with their developed skills, or a crisis state suddenly occurs. For example, perhaps in the past your child may have experienced their cousin visiting as an experience that ended in their nervous system being in a crisis state. Due to the relationship you have developed and the cornerstones providing security and stability, when the cousin visits, your child now knows to 'keep themselves and others safe' and tells their cousin to 'stop' when they don't like their actions, before coming to sit with you. This different way of communication has the same intentions as when your child's nervous system has previously been in crisis and their communication would have been to strike out at their cousin in a bid to get them to stop.

Maybe you are out with friends at a familiar environment and your child has usually been happy and regulated there but on this occasion the environment is not meeting their needs. They tell you they have had enough and want to leave so you reply, 'In a few minutes,' and your child goes back to playing. Seeing your child is playing again, you continue talking to your friend and the time creeps on. Suddenly your child is in a crisis state and instinctively you know you should have left with them when they requested to do so. Your child may have been managing these activities with increased skills, but they were not experiencing the activities differently. Your child had managed to communicate their needs to you but you have interpreted this as that they are regulated, when actually they are still overwhelmed but able to recognise and communicate this to you. Previously they would have shown their overwhelm through behaviour changes that you would then act on so they did not reach crisis point.

Communication is not always straightforward or displayed in a direct explicit manner; often when a child or adult is overwhelmed or in crisis, the communication is not a true reflection of their nervous system state. Your child may express 'no' as 'I hate you', a shrug of the shoulders could mean 'okay'. 'I don't know,' could be a means of communicating they are not ready for discussion just yet, throwing items could be a means of changing the environment around them. None of this miscommunication is intentional, your child's nervous system is seeking a predictable outcome or to regain control of the environment to assist with restoring their balance.

It is through building your relationship and developing the understanding of the nervous system states that you can learn the true intention of your child's communication. Navigating discussions when the child is regulated to clarify the meaning of their future responses allows you to develop strategies that provide the safety and predictability that your child seeks. It is crucial for your child's emotional well-being and long-term development, that they have people around them that they can connect with on a deeper level, who grant them autonomy and validate their experiences.

Understanding the complexities of the nervous system states is crucial to providing effective support to your child. Embracing your child's unique autistic way of being fosters trust and understanding that enables you to recognise their true signs of regulation, overwhelm and crisis, enabling you to meet their needs with compassion and empathy. Parenting is not about perfection, it is about connecting with your child, reflecting on the days gone by and developing your skills for the future.

# 3.2 – FROM CHAOS TO CALM

*Amidst the chaos, our devoted support becomes the bridge that guides them from turbulent storms to tranquil shores, where serenity and strength await.*

It almost feels impossible. Even with all the things you have learnt, your child still has times that they are in crisis and you spend hours attempting to regulate them, trying to get back to a point where life can continue. You have put the four cornerstones in place; your home has structure and routines, you have implemented visuals and you allow for transitions. Yet your child still appears to be overwhelmed, teetering on the edge of crisis.

I want to tell you that it is possible. It is possible to get to a point where your child and you spend the majority of your time in a regulated state. That isn't to say there won't ever be any crisis or overwhelmed moments, but

I am saying it is possible to reduce the amount of time it takes for your child to come out of crisis state. It is possible for your child to recognise they have become overwhelmed and seek the support that provides the predictability they crave, and it is possible for you and your child to have a relationship that enables this to happen. Let's explore how you can achieve these things.

**Time**
As parents we often feel like there is not enough time in the day; housework, careers, shopping, relationships all take time from us. Time is intangible, subject to interpretation and constantly moves forward but the elusive concept of time is vital to supporting your child. You can spend your time supporting your child through crisis because their needs have not been met, or instead you can spend the time meeting their needs, validating their experiences and sharing a connection. Either way your child will require your time.

Making time to actively be truly present with your child when they are regulated, shows you value their companionship and builds strong emotional connections. Giving your time to join your child in activities of their choosing will create opportunities for meaningful communication and promote a sense of security. Giving time within all of your cornerstones, building time in to your structure and routines, allowing the time for transitions and the use of visuals will all help to reduce anxiety, teach your child they can rely on you to be consistent and provide the predictability they require.

When your child is overwhelmed, remembering to

give additional time for them to process, respond and function indicates that you understand their needs. Sometimes this is shown by 'holding space' for them - being silent in the same room, not forcing connection or communication, just being present and available. Our child describes time when her nervous system is overwhelmed as 'paralysing'. If she is aware of time passing by, of things needing to be done, then she becomes paralysed by the sense of urgency within her and is prevented from functioning by her own operating system. When your child is overwhelmed, try to respect their boundaries, offer reassurance and comfort in ways your child responds to when regulated. Be present and available without imposing yourself, while being mindful of any cues from them that they are seeking support or communication. Giving time to your child when they are overwhelmed is a compassionate and effective means of supporting their nervous system and development.

During a crisis state, your child's and your own safety must always be the priority concern. Time is still an essential consideration. You can provide time to your child during a crisis state by being mindful of how you present to them. Try not to show you are clock-watching, avoid appearing impatient. You can provide your child with time by not allowing your focus to be pulled away, whether that be by a phone call, your own thoughts or another family member. Expecting your child to stop the crisis and be obedient or coercing them with comments like, 'If you don't come now, dinner will be ruined', is likely to destroy trust and build your child's anxiety. In these crisis moments your child is your priority. Consider if you can get someone to take over cooking or switch off and delay the cooking. Put your phone away on silent, allow the other children extra time at their activity while you support this child. Giving time in crisis provides a sense of calm and control. Your child needs to feel there is no hidden agenda, that you are not just telling them it is okay; they need to truly feel it is okay to take the time they need. Your child needs time for their nervous system to restore and be able to function and the amount of time this takes will vary depending on the factors that led to the crisis and the support that is given.

When you have provided your child with time during a crisis state and their nervous system has become more balanced, you both then need time to recover and rest. Crisis is an exhausting and often scary state; do not rush this recovery process, everything else can wait. Having rest and recovery time together after a state of crisis will demonstrate empathy, provide space for your child to express themselves and allow opportunities for communication. There have been many moments over the last decade that my child and I have spent hours in their bedroom, initially in crisis, then in recovery, with no expectation for them to rejoin our family. Our structure provides the basis the family needs, we focus on keeping everyone safe and fed, routines and transitions for the child are firmly supported or reduced if possible, and visuals are used to support communication and reduce misunderstandings.

**Honour**
To truly support our children we must also honour their needs. Honouring involves accepting and respecting their

individual development, their presentation and their unique personality throughout all their nervous system responses. For example, it is not enough to accept that your child likes to jump excitedly when they are regulated but when they are in crisis and jump about to an extreme, to tell them not to do it for fear of societal repercussions. Your child has the need to jump. This may be to meet a sensory need or to assist with processing and they may find doing this when in crisis is a strategy that assists their nervous system to restore. Being prevented from jumping will prevent your child from innately meeting their need and it also takes away their autonomy.

Honour your child's needs at every opportunity. If they ask a thousand questions, try and answer as many as possible (as patiently as you can manage!) This will support them to find the reassurance or knowledge that they seek. Allow your child to choose not to join in with activities if they express this is not for them. It may be they do not want to join the family game night or do not feel able to sit outside with the family when having a BBQ. Try and have a backup option, it may be that your child does a separate activity but choses to be nearby, or perhaps they eat inside because the outside area is too bright for them. Allow your child to express their individuality without fear of repercussions, sometimes as a parent you may feel your child will become disrespectful if you allow them to do as they request at each and every opportunity, however, your structure provides the principles and boundaries to keep you all safe. By allowing your child opportunities to respectfully express their needs you can model healthy means of expression. Your child needs to know you acknowledge their displeasures as much as their pleasures; it might be you are a football fan and your child has no interest or perhaps they want to dance but you feel that they have little chance of succeeding and see it as pointless. Try to move past your own views and see the excitement your child has and the need to express their own personality. Your child needs to know you will support their passions and interests even if these differ from your own preferences or expectations.

Honour your child's need to leave situations before you do. Teach them a get out clause, keywords that mean you know they need to leave quickly. For our children 'I'm done' gets them out of the situation immediately, no questions asked. We respect their preferred means of communication and remember this may change as their needs vary. For many children using visual aids like pictures or written words via text can assist the communication when overwhelmed and offer an alternative to verbal input being received. When your child is finding it difficult to focus on a task that is required, offering to body double is a supportive way to acknowledge their needs. Body doubling requires you to be nearby, not actively participating, but providing a supportive presence while the child completes the task. Allowing your child to have passive activities also supports their needs. Passive activities require minimal engagement and little mental or physical effort, the TV playing in the background, daydreaming, videos on multiple screens, music via headphones. Yes, this may mean you need to text your child or physically be in front of them to gain their attention because they are creating the stimuli they require to maintain regulation, but you are showing you respect their need to have this input.

When you honour your child's needs at every opportunity, you demonstrate to them your understanding and unconditional support for their autistic way of being and you proactively support your child to express themselves; you are providing your child with autonomy within a safe and supportive environment.

**Restore**
Providing your child with a consistent sense of calm, comfort and stability, regardless of their nervous system state, is a powerful way of restoring their balance. You are laying the foundations for a secure attachment that will offer your child ongoing security this will become an integral part of their development as they internalise and replicate this attachment throughout life. Restoring your child's balance often, will provide a healthy model from which your child will also learn nervous system self-care, tailored to their unique needs.

You may wonder how you can restore when your child is in the regulated state. Restoring when regulated is taking action to reduce the likelihood of overwhelm or crisis; it is providing a nurturing presence that maintains the regulated state and pre-emptively reduces potential triggers. Imagine seeing rain clouds in the sky. You are not anticipating a storm, but still you bring in the washing off the line and close the windows - you take action to restore the balance in case it rains. Restoring when a child is regulated improves their overall wellbeing, you increase their awareness of feel-good factors, foster trust, acknowledge how regulated presents for them and in doing so you teach them the nervous state to return to. A child whose balance is often restored when regulated is more likely to feel secure and able to explore with curiosity and confidence. Activities that restore your child's balance will be unique to them but can include the opportunity for movement, rest and connection with yourself. Perhaps your child likes having their arms stroked while reading a book or bouncing with you on the trampoline and attempting to make you fall. Ensuring you spend time with your child each day doing these activities helps to restore their balance. It may be your child finds making vocal sounds or sucking their thumb a means of relaxing or perhaps listening to music, reading or being in nature. Any activities of relaxation and pleasure, solely or with others, also boost the balance and restore a sense of individuality and acceptance. When you act with and for your child in their regulated state you are restoring their balance; it may be ensuring they are hydrated, providing a yoga ball for them to bounce on, watching their favourite program with them for the thousandth time or going for a walk together. As long as what you do optimises your child's functioning and feelings of contentment then you are taking pre-emptive steps to counteract the impact overwhelm and crisis can create.

If we think back to that storm but this time, there is no forewarning. The rain suddenly pours and you are caught in the middle of it. You cannot dry out while still in the storm; You need to change the environment or wait for the storm to pass. It is the same for your child when they are overwhelmed. To restore the balance within an overwhelmed nervous state there needs to be a focus on reducing the triggers and providing an improved sensory-friendly environment. These actions will provide feelings of safety, allow your child a sense of control and will facilitate the regulation of the nervous system.

A child's overwhelm does not always appear as could be expected; it may present as a need for attention from others, as seeking control within the situation or as a sensory seeking behaviour often classified as being hyperactive. During overwhelm you can help to restore the balance by reducing the overstimulating input given to your child, increasing activities of pleasure and utilising tools that assist when in the state of regulation. For example modelling deep breathing using blowing bubbles or counting breaths in and out, are good tools to assist with deep breathing. I used to encourage our children to visualise and pretend to smell the flowers and then blow out the candles on a cake. For your child it maybe you need to encourage the use of a weighted or sensory blanket to offer deep pressure or tactile feedback. Fidgets or the opportunity to bounce on a yoga ball can satisfy the need for movement. Performing grounding techniques, for example, 5, 4, 3, 2 1 where you name 5 things you can see, 4 things you can feel, 3 things you can hear, 2 things you can smell and 1 thing you can taste. This technique brings your child's attention back to the present moment. You may need to adapt this exercise for your child and do only one for each sense. Our child does not like to do this if we count, but if I discuss what I can see she joins in and this helps to restore her balance. These strategies will need to be modelled to your child throughout the differing nervous system states until they become a natural response for your child to use independently.

A thunderstorm. Unpredictable, electrifying. No surety of how long the thunder will roar or when it will truly be finished. This is our crisis state. Science says the most dangerous time is just before and after a thunderstorm. We know 'before' can happen so quickly that moving to safety is sometimes impossible. As the distance between the flashes of lightening and the roar of the thunder grows, people feel safe once again until a sudden flash of lightening reminds them the storm is still ongoing. This is akin to your child restoring their balance; they may no longer be screaming, physically lashing out or fiercely sobbing so there becomes an assumption that your child's nervous system is now in a regulated state. Most likely your child is not regulated; they have simply, like the thunderstorm dissipated, slightly.

When your child's nervous system is in a crisis state they need their balance restored via an environment that meets their need, there needs to be an immediate reduction of triggers and the safety of everyone involved needs to be paramount. This may mean you ask everyone else in the room to leave or you guide the child from the area to a safe space. You will need to reduce as much external stimuli and input as possible and increase supportive tools, for example, comfort items. During crisis, support can be provided in the form of an increased sensory- friendly environment, grounding techniques, and offering comfort and reassurance while respecting boundaries and communication preferences. Sometimes, even with the use of these tools, the storm must pass by of its own accord.

Once the storm has passed the focus needs to move first to rest and recovery before returning to a regulated state. Rest and recovery during the crisis stage may mean moving your child to a place of physical comfort, perhaps a favourite spot on the sofa or a bean bag in their bedroom. Your child may need to nap, eat or drink during this stage, you would be best to let them do so as their nervous system will likely be exhausted and needs to replenish its energy. During this time you could also provide activities that promote relaxation for your child; this may be soothing music, cuddles, comfort items or colouring. When your child is able to engage appropriately for them, they may be able to express what helped and underlying triggers could possibly be addressed to aid with the transitioning. Restoration of balance is needed, however, before your child can transition to the regulated state.

Restoring the balance then, is not about alleviating the displayed behaviours in that moment, it is about bringing calm to a chaotic nervous system, optimising functioning and allowing processing and responses to happen at your child's naturally required pace. Restoration is vital at each nervous system stage to improve your child's overall wellbeing whilst also teaching acceptance of self-care strategies that aid rest and recovery.

**Innovate**
To support your child with every nervous system

stage you will also need to be innovative. Innovation involves being experimental, creative and being willing to take risks to achieve progress. This can be done in a pre-emptive manner, planning for situations that might arise. For example, we were creative in teaching our children the keywords 'purple pineapples' for communicating a need to us covertly. The words are catchy and easy to remember, there is no literal interpretation as purple pineapples cannot actually be bought. Only our family, not our social circle or wider circle know the meaning of these words. Let me show you how we use it.

If our child is, for example, visiting a friend's house where they are happy and content but then the situation changes, maybe their friend's sibling has returned home which causes our child to feel uncomfortable. She does not want to explain to her friend or for her friend to know, but they are in the room so she is able to call me and will drop into our conversation, 'Did you get purple pineapples?' I can respond with, 'Yes, I bought fifteen'. Our child then knows I will be there in fifteen minutes; I will take responsibility for getting them out of the situation. This pro-active strategy was devised when our child was anxious to visit new places. Even though she wanted to spend time with friends, the thought of being trapped in an uncomfortable situation, unable to express her needs for fear of upsetting her friend, could cause her to miss out on going.

There may be other times where you will need to innovate more in the moment. Perhaps you are out of the home and your child would usually use their blanket as a tool to restore their balance but you did not bring it. Maybe your hoodie wrapped snugly around their neck could create the same sensation for them or perhaps putting the socks you have on over their socks will provide the extra pressure they seek which would usually come from the blanket. Perhaps the blanket usually serves the purpose of a hiding place, so maybe a towel could create a similar hiding place.

Incorporating your child's interests into a situation can also help to ease tension, sometimes your autistic child may feel an innate demand to comply with societal or external expectations and this can lead to feelings of frustration and anxiety. Bringing in a favourite character as a third party can often de-escalate the demand your child may feel. We once arrived at the school playground with our child's pet snake as a means of reintegrating her to the school environment after a period of absence. The other children were thrilled to see a live snake in the playground, the teachers, not so much!

There may be occasions you want to praise or express feelings to your child but you feel this may trigger their nervous system and so you need to be innovative in your approach. Some children feel discomfort receiving praise and this may be because past experiences have drawn unwanted attention to them. For some, praise may create feelings of overwhelm or induce anxiety that there is now an expectation on the child to always meet this standard. Making observations and commenting on your child's uniqueness can help to build a strong parent- child connection and deliver praise in a less direct manner. For example, 'You have so many creative ideas' or 'I love your passion for...'. By making feedback individualised, '(name) I love your sass when you stand firm in your beliefs,' you are showing genuine appreciation for your child. It may be that your child responds well to humour so you could purposefully create a situation in which they can laugh, or that using alternative communication methods such as text-based apps, artificial intelligence or visuals allows you to present these thoughts to your child. These methods can also encourage your child to express their feelings and needs while fostering autonomy and independence. Tailoring innovative approaches specific to your child's needs fosters a supportive environment that respects individuality. Not only will you assist your child to navigate challenging situations with confidence, but you will also develop a relationship of acceptance and understanding.

**Validate**
Autistic children can often feel dismissed, different or like they are always wrong. Your child therefore needs you as their safe person to validate the way they are experiencing life. Your child's responses are directly linked to their neurosensory experiences, so it is crucial that you cultivate a home that is non-judgemental towards your child's differences and avoids language that criticises such as, 'you're overreacting' or, 'you should be able to do this'. To validate experiences, you need to focus on supporting without judgement; creating an atmosphere of trust where your child can openly express themselves without fear.

'I understand this is really hard for you right now' or 'It's okay to feel upset.'

These are both comments that will validate your child's experience.

To create trust between you, involve your child in decision making and problem-solving, together you can brainstorm strategies or tools that may help address your child 's experiences.  You could ask your child what specifically causes them distress in the home environment and model adapting the environment for them. This could be installing blinds if the natural light is too strong in the morning, asking for the TV volume to be reduced on an evening or making another slice of toast if the butter tastes funny. Regularly practising validation during times when your child is regulated can empower your child to identify what supports them during times of crisis or overwhelm.

It is important to validate your child's experiences when they say they cannot do something; this is often not a 'will not' do it, but a genuine innate feeling of 'can't'. Validate their experience, if your child cannot go in the bathroom for fear of spiders being in there, check the bathroom for them each time. If your child has enjoyed a family trip out bowling before but now says they can't, validate that. Using the WISE approach we explored earlier in Part 2.2 may help you to figure out the cause of their inability to do the activity.  For example, when this happened with our child, I realised that during the last experience we had at the bowling centre there was a large, loud group playing in the next lane which created an experience of displeasure for her. She now anticipates this same situation happening if bowling is mentioned.

Summarising what your child has said to you is a means of demonstrating that you understand their experience and give value to how they sense the world around them. Summarising involves consolidating the main points of your child's communication and reflecting their feelings back, while providing appreciation of their willingness to share with you and clarifying that your version aligns with their experience. When you summarise what your child has communicated like this, you show that you are actively listening to their feelings and thoughts which provides the validation of their experiences.

Teaching your child the power of 'Stop' is a means of validating their individual experience. In this example, 'Stop' is used when two people are touching each other, your child and the co-parent are playing together, tickling each other to create laughter. Your child wants to continue playing but the co-parent has verbally said 'stop', they have raised their hands in the air to symbolise Stop and they are no longer touching your child. This experience can develop into a means of teaching how to keep oneself safe as the co-parent can create a distance between the child and themselves using a cushion as a barrier if your child does not stop. You can model that the co-parent does not want to be touched. You can explicitly explain that they verbally said stop and showed this by raising their hands in the motion of stop, much like the traffic warden does on the way to school to stop the vehicles. A child who is taught the power of stop is then able to use this to validate their own experiences. Perhaps in the play gym, another child throws balls at them. At first, your child throws balls back but when one ball hits your child particularly hard your child states 'stop'. If the other child continues and your child knows through previous experience they can create a distance and leave the situation with no judgement from you, they are more likely to validate their own experience and move to safety.

Validating your child is also about listening to them when they express themselves to you without dismissing their experience or displaying annoyance as they seek understanding. If your child believes in something then so can you - we have charged crystals by storms, left food for the reindeers and walked across bridges like penguins because it validates their experience.

It can be difficult when a child used to present in a particular manner during a nervous system state and now appears to present differently, as explained in part 3.1 this is an increase in skills. Try not to view this as a negative; the relationship you are building with your child will be allowing them to truly be themselves in your presence and it's important to view this new presentation with positivity. Focus on the achievements; your child used to scream and damage items when in crisis but now they maintain safety and explain the required activity is too much. This new presentation needs to be validated with identical respect, as the experience they are having is the same; it is your child's expression that has changed, their skills that have developed. Everyone experiences the world around them differently and it's important that you give value to your child's experience in all situations. Sometimes, say if this is between siblings, it can be hard to validate each experience when they are together. Perhaps the experience is siblings disagreeing over who had an item first. You may need to separately discuss the experience with each of them before bringing everyone together to figure out a way forward that shows understanding and acceptance to all involved.

Validate your child without boundaries. Teach them that your love is unconditional and irrelevant to their nervous system state. Modelling kindness and empathy towards them in each state will make positive contributions to your child's wellbeing. Tell them that they are a valued member of the family, that their experiences count and thank them for sharing them with you. Validating your child's experiences embraces their uniqueness and differences, while installing a sense of acceptance and self-worth.

**Environment**
By incorporating the four cornerstones into your home you have been creating an environment that can best meet the needs of your child. You will have begun to centre your focus on developing a holistic environment that proactively supports your child's unique, autistic way of being. But there is still more to do. To maintain the environment you have created you will need to regularly communicate and connect with all of the family to ensure everyone feels valued and able to express themselves; this will foster understanding, empathy and open communication within your home environment. Celebrating strengths and progress over challenges and unmet milestones, will empower acceptance and understanding. You can now also discuss with the people in your social circles about your child's needs, set

boundaries for them explaining the meaning of what the values are in your home and welcoming them to learn how to step on the pathway into your safe space if they want to be included in the environment you create for your child.

Think about the sensory adaptions your child needs to their environment and how this may change throughout the differing nervous system states, incorporate sensory strategies into your weekly structure and daily routines. There are multiple environments to consider within your home, outside areas, inside – personal and communal spaces. It is essential that you try to provide an environment that meets your child's sensory divergence; this may be having a swing chair in your living room, weighted blankets and fluffy covers rather than duvets. It may mean using soft lightening or LEDs around the house rather than traditional light bulbs. Perhaps your child needs time outside each day, or maybe they need time without technology and to have a dancing session instead. It may be your child requires a trampoline in the house or a trip to the park for a swing daily. It may be the lights bother your child and so you could change to dimmer light switches. It could be you keep a large bean bag handy for the crisis states or a box of fidgets accessible in every room at all times.

Pick your battles and look at the bigger picture. If it helps your child's nervous system to stay regulated then can they dress in front of the TV, wear shorts in the snow or use an iPad before bed? Consider if you can you make their environment more comfortable, reliable and less confusing by allowing these things to happen. It may be helpful to think about what you can provide daily to help your child feel at ease in the home environment and maintain a regulated state. We use headphones, fidgets, blankets, communication via text, visuals, personalised strategies of support and routines tailored to the childrens' needs. We adjust the environment to meet their needs; for the child who likes the breeze her window is constantly open, for the child who dislikes bugs, her window is closed to reduce the chances of flies. One child functions in a room that appears messy but to her is comfortable, this is allowed with the only expectation being it is kept safe. Another child needs everything to be in its place and has a very organised room. The kitchen and living room are the usual rooms to consume food, however, if needed, food can be eaten in their personal rooms. We also keep ear defenders and bean bags around for times of overwhelm. We teach self- awareness and have support available at all times. During crisis we do all of this and adapt routines, lower demands, and provide calm, consistent support as a team. Be aware what is manageable for your child in one state may not be in another. Adapt the environment as their needs and state change, blow out the candles and turn down the music, flick your phone on to silent. Reduce what you can to create a calming environment that respects their neuro and sensory needs.

During this chapter you have learnt about giving **T**ime, **H**onouring needs, **R**estoring the balance, being **I**nnovative, **V**alidating experiences and adapting the **E**nvironment. These are the six key elements to supporting your child throughout the nervous system states of being regulated, overwhelmed or in crisis. This approach is how you support your child to **THRIVE**. The elements do not change depending on the state but the means by which we deliver the support, does. Using the **THRIVE** approach during regulation will assist you to build a toolkit of strategies to support your child during overwhelm and crisis that are familiar and reassuring to them. Using the **THRIVE** approach during overwhelm and crisis will provide the calm, consistent, reassuring support your child needs to be able to return to a regulated state.

# 3.3 – YOUR VOICE COUNTS

*If conforming sparks chaos and autonomy ignites opportunity, then advocacy needs to fuel the empowerment.*

The culture of our society promotes conforming and is resistant to any deviation from the accepted norm. Your child will often challenge this status quo. It is important as their parent you guide them to trust their inner voice and listen to their instincts for what is right for them. Earlier in the book we considered the importance of letting go of perfect; it's time to abandon the expectation to conform that has stifled your own authenticity and parenting. Your child needs you to stop comparing them and trying to fit them in to an idealised standard and instead help them to develop their own unique autistic way of being. If you can grant your child autonomy and utilise the power of advocacy then you will open doors to endless possibilities, diversity and individuality.

There is a delicate balance between providing guidance and support and allowing autonomy. To clarify, autonomy is respecting your child's ability to make choices and decisions within their own capabilities. No one on the outside sees how hard you work as a parent to stay connected to your child; the complexities of the collaboration between you are often invisible. The single-lens approach others view your parent-child collaboration with, often does not allow them to see the conscious effort you put in to supporting your child's autonomy, allowing autonomy is confused with 'giving in.'

Allowing autonomy can appear in the simplest of forms. It can be asking which shoes your child wants to wear, giving a choice of cereals at breakfast or accepting their opinion that they do not need a coat. It's asking if they require your assistance rather than assuming they do. It is respecting their voice and their choice at each and every opportunity.

Each night I have the opportunity to take autonomy away from my child, she requires her blankets to be laid in a way that feels just right to her. This can often mean the three blankets she uses laid five or six times until they feel just right. I could tell her after the second or third attempt that the blankets would have to suffice, that I will not continue to readjust the blankets time and time again. But I don't. I allow her the autonomy to tell me when they are comfortable. We have built the time this blanket-balancing takes into our routine. I honour her need to re-do the blankets and this restores the balance to keep her regulated. We have had to be innovative in our approach to adjusting the environment. We now place the blankets in silence with no distractions to create an opportunity for the best experience. I respect her ability to know what is right for her and in doing so, she puts her trust in me to support and advocate for her.

The autistic experience makes daily living more intense, more overwhelming, more unpredictable so it makes sense that an autistic person may need more time to rest, reflect, create, connect, process and play. But how do you manage to encourage these opportunities within a society that places expectations on your child to develop and progress at a set rate? You can challenge these rigid expectations and advocate for more inclusive and flexible approaches that account for diverse ways of being. Advocacy is not just speaking up about an issue. Advocacy is enacting a meaningful change; taking steps to promote awareness of the issues and activate support. Advocacy is ensuring your autistic child has the resources and support to enable them to thrive.

What does advocacy look like in your life? Throughout this book you have learnt to advocate for your child within your home, you have created meaningful change, taken steps to support your child's needs. You now provide the resources and support to help your child thrive within your home. To be able to show you how to actively advocate for your child within society we need to step outside of the boundaries of your home.

In the last chapter you learnt the acronym **THRIVE** to

help support your child throughout the nervous system states. The same acronym can be used to advocate for your child in society. You can advocate that your child needs **T**ime, that their needs have to be **H**onoured, that the balance needs to be **R**estored before being able to move forward. You can advocate for **I**nnovative methods of support, encourage those in yours circles to think outside the societal box to enable your child's experience to be **V**alidated and the **E**nvironment adapted. You know you can support your child to thrive, advocating is about helping and equipping other people with the knowledge to do the same.

Children are expected by societal developmental measures to be self-sufficient at certain ages but in reality this is not always the case. Often this is where the gap of difference starts to be noted between your child and similar aged peers. Society downplays the significance of transitions and events by minimizing the impact that can be seen. For example, children are expected to accept visitors and trips with little notice of changes to their routine, the transition to high school is often supported with just one day visit, but inwardly for some children these are huge events for which they may need time to process and adjust before being able to partake. Show your child they do not need to follow the societal norms, take the pressure away from them and teach them it's ok to have time to adjust and take time to accomplish.

There have been many occasions in the school playground the teachers would appear, the lines would form and my child would still be close to me. As the other children went inside the teachers would catch my eye and before they had the opportunity to tell me she would be fine once she had gone in to school, I would tell them, 'I will knock on the door once she is ready'. You see, 'fine' for my child meant she would have put on a mask and was containing her overwhelm. Rather than letting her have to do that, I would sit with my child and give her the time she needed until the balance was restored in her nervous system. If staff approached, I would validate my child's experience and ensure they were prepared to honour her need. I ensured my child was given the time she needed to process and function.

It may also be helpful to advocate for your child when making health appointments. You can explain your child's needs and ask for a longer appointment. It may be useful to search for different settings that are more able to meet your child's needs. The opticians we visit is a small local practice, they willingly book us a double appointment so we can arrive a few minutes after their last client and we can leave before the next one arrives. When we go to the dentist now there is only one particular dentist our children will see, they have a calming and caring demeanour and never rush the children. We only arrange appointments for when they are available. When we had to rush to A & E for a suspected broken wrist I advocated for my child's needs. We were given a smaller quieter room to wait in than the larger busy waiting area.

Give your child the time when you are out in the community with making decisions, for example queuing at an ice cream shop. Who is more important - your child or the person behind you in the queue tutting impatiently? Be respectfully assertive. I always find thanking people in advance of what you want them to do is helpful to the situation. In this scenario I would say, "Thank you for your understanding, we just need a little more time," before returning my focus to my child. Don't be afraid to request additional time in social situations, in most instances people are unaware this is required but are happy to accommodate. You may also find it helpful to advocate for your child's needs when you are supporting them with involvement in social activities. Perhaps it would help your child if you arrived to football practice five minutes early so they can transition before the hustle and bustle of the team arriving, or that your child is given time to observe and process the requirements of the activity before it is their turn. Again, people are usually happy to accommodate and include your child but aren't aware this may be needed. Taking time to explain and suggest the approaches that may support your child is advocating not only for them but also opens people's awareness of inclusion.

Honour your child's needs when in public just like you would in the home; your child needs the consistency that you will advocate for them in all spaces. When you are visiting somewhere, anticipate potential challenges and plan the visit in advance. Most places have an accessibility section on their website or can explain their accessible options when spoken to. Seek to find the information you need before attending, you know your child's needs and triggers, use the support provided to meet their need and reduce their triggers. Use the carers pass to enable you to reduce the queue time. Ask for the key to the accessible toilet so your child is not surrounded by other people and triggered by the sounds of the hand dryers. Request the music to be turned down in the seating area or for a different table that better meets your child's needs. Advocate when your social circle wants to spend time with you, maybe going out for dinner is a monthly routine but on this particular day your child is overwhelmed; honour their need for rest and recovery over time with the social circle. When you have had previous positive experiences with your social circle it is hard to set boundaries and place your child's needs first but this will happen at some point as your child's need change. Those in your social circle who are your tribe and truly understand what you are going through will still be available when your child's needs allow joint experiences again.

Advocating for your child means that you are communicating what they need, it may not always be what you want. However, it is their body and their experience and so it needs to be their choice. If they do not want the yearly photo taking (as much as you may want it to go with your collection) withdraw your consent and honour their need to not partake. When an issue is raised to you from a setting outside of the home you can use the **WISE** approach to explore the issues by asking: **W**hen did this become an issue, is it a recurring recent thing or has it happened on a few intermittent occasions? Perhaps there has become an issue since the peer at their side changed. Is it the **I**ndividual need, is your child being required to use skills they do not yet have? Maybe your child needs to sit at the back of the group so as not to fear other children touching them, but is currently sat in the middle of a row. Is it the **S**equence of events? Has the routine been changed by the setting, are they forgetting a key event within the sequence? Is your child now required to sit in an uncomfortable position for longer? Or is it the Environment, has their seat been changed or does it need to be adjusted? **Be WISE** and advocate for the change that honours your child's needs.

At every opportunity of advocacy, clarify your child's expectations; do they have the same understanding as you do? Collaborate together how you will restore the balance and advocate their voice to those involved. If we consider the football team, it could be your child feels they need the chance to restore alone at half time rather than being in the changing room with the team. Advocate for this to happen and help be part of the solution, offer to meet your child as they come off the pitch or request staff support them during this time. In certain situations, for example at school, breaks are given as playtimes throughout the day in an attempt to restore the balance. However, for autistic children these play times do not equal a chance to restore the balance; a break that is forced or given when not needed can feel like a demand. A break that implies the need to continue to socialise, is not a chance to rest and recover. If this is the case for your child then try advocating for your child to have individual small breaks when needed, for this break to include activities that help them to restore. Explain to the relevant people that these breaks that meet their need will allow your child a chance to restore, create autonomy, build trust and reduce instances of overwhelm and crisis for your child.

I am not saying it is easy to advocate; chances are you

may need to become, *'that parent'*. You will need to step out of your comfort zone and ooze an authority and self-assurance that may crumble the moment you are alone. But your voice counts! To successfully advocate for your child, you will need to be innovative in your approach. Your child is unique and you will need to tailor the solutions you propose to your child's needs and strengths. Sometimes people want to help and do the things your child needs, but they misunderstand the communication and what you are aiming for. Sometimes people may create resistance to the change you are asking for because they cannot visualise how it will assist. Do not be put off. Keep advocating.

On one occasion on a family day out, during a crisis moment in the middle of a theme park, I advocated for my child with the security guard, telling them that we needed to get out of the busy environment and return to our car. I asked if they could help and received a negative response with very little support. So, with my child very visibly in crisis, I didn't give up and asked for their manager. When their manager arrived, they asked what I needed and within minutes there was a golf buggy at our side and they were more than happy to give our child and I a lift out of the overwhelming theme park. Sometimes you have to be persistent and creative to get the support you need.

During all of your advocacy it is vital that you continue to validate your child's experience. There have been times I have been called to the school for an issue surrounding my child's behaviour. I listen to the information given to me by the staff and validate the experience of the events, then I ask for time alone with my child. I create a safe environment for my child to discuss with me and ask my child about their experience. I validate their experience, my child is reassured that I do not judge them and my child knows that only when I have discovered their experience, will I work with others to find a way forward.

Advocate for your child's experience to be validated when in public with others. It is so common for people to unintentionally dismiss an experience because it is not a trigger to them. This is often the case when a child comes to tell you of an altercation between peers and well-meaning adults will respond with, 'oh they didn't mean to, go back and play'. Validate your child's experience - if this altercation means they no longer want to play with the peer, accept it and advocate so your child knows you will protect them.

It can be difficult as a parent to stop the automatic move into 'fix it' mode when a situation arises, especially if accepted social conventions are ignored, but the situation that happened may not always be as a person has implied it to you. Your child needs to know you will have their back outside of the home and that you will allow them to share how they experienced the situation in question. They need to know that you will validate their experience and hold space for them when the experience has impacted their nervous system. What your child needs most is for you not to jump to conclusions but to validate their worth and investigate the unmet need that led to the experience.

It is just as important to validate your child's experiences which have brought them pleasure and advocate for more of these. That may mean that the social circle takes your child to the same place every occasion you spend time together. If this supports your child and allows the occasion to happen then this is the way it needs to be. Advocate to those who want to be involved in your child's life that they need to be prepared to use the **THRIVE** approach in the best interests of your child. There may be occasions where you need to validate your social circles experiences and help them to be **WISE**. They will not support your child as effectively as you do all the time but the effort they put in to being with your child and supporting you massively counts; if they are trying and attempting to learn then hold on to these people and keep teaching. For those who are unprepared to use the **THRIVE** approach for your family, consider your own experiences and those of your family - is the detriment that you feel from their involvement, worth the experience that you have with this social circle, or do you perhaps need to consider new boundaries. You may perhaps find it helpful to set a boundary that you travel in your own vehicle when going out together so that you can leave the environment when it no longer meets your child's needs? Or it may be that you only agree to meeting in particular venues that you know will accommodate your family's differences.

Think about the environments you take your child to, advocate and plan for your family not other families. Be kind to yourself, there may be environments that your whole family will never be able to attend, this is okay. There could be occasions you need to separate as a family as a strategy to meet differing needs, advocate for this to happen; teach your family and those in your circles it's better for this to happen as it helps to meet differing needs. Think ahead when changing environments, try to anticipate triggers for your child and advocate to get these reduced, maybe the social circle always has the TV on loud as you enter, could you ask for the volume to be muted as you arrive. Advocate for the environments to meet everyone's needs not just the need of one person. You may need to have the car radio off as standard or ensure a choice of music that can be managed by all, it may be you allow ear buds and personal music in the car. Advocate at every opportunity for your child's needs to be met in the moment; take snacks and drinks, keep resources that are used to restore the balance available while you are out and about and use them without the fear of judgement from society.

Think about other environments and how these differ from yours. Is your home one of calm and routine with very few visitors, but then a visit to the social circles house consists of people in and out, with background noise and lots of shouting. Consider how long your child can manage in that environment, advocate for adaptions to be made that can reduce potential of overwhelm or crisis for your child. This may mean you advocate that the weekly visit to the social circle is reduced from an afternoon to an hour, but if this helps your child maintain the balance of regulation it will be worth it.

Do not expect your child to conform to meet the needs of others, this creates chaos and encourages your child to mask and ignore their internal needs. Allow your child to see the advocation in the moment; discuss with them why you have advocated, explain your reasons, and ask if they feel it helped. Give your child the opportunity to express how you could have handled the situation differently. Laugh with them and devise new ways you can advocate in future. Go to the extreme and the impossible. Ask them which way they feel is best for you to advocate next time. Perhaps ask how they would advocate, if there is anything you could do to support them to advocate for themselves.

When you make advocating for their needs a daily part of living it will encourage your child to advocate for themselves. Most children will need to practise this skill and home will likely be the place they feel comfortable to attempt this. Try and recognise when you child is attempting to do this and avoid dismissing your child's advocation because it feels like a challenge to your parenting. Allowing children to learn to make choices and guiding them to hone the skill of advocation means they arrive at adulthood well-practiced and able to place boundaries if their needs are not honoured.

Self-advocacy is critical to being able to protect oneself. Develop your child's awareness of their autistic way of being, make plans to support them to achieve and implement self-advocacy and develop their strength in doing so daily. We recently had a professional visit our house. Before the visit our child expressed that they wanted me to be present. However, we also discussed how the child could advocate if they wanted me to leave the room. Knowing that our child prefers subtle communication rather than directly telling me to leave, it was agreed she would tell me I could go make a coffee.

This allowed our child the chance to advocate for time with the professional on her own in a way that met her needs.

Using your child's intrinsic motivation to encourage self advocation can also be successful. Once, in the middle of September our child had been talking about Christmas all week. Eventually she managed to explain that she had been thinking about this for the past few days but not wanting to voice it out loud due to societal expectations holding her back. "I really want to put my Christmas tree up." At this point as parents we could have laughed at this seemingly unreasonable request of having a Christmas tree up in the middle of September, knowing that it is more conventional do this later in the year. Our child loves Christmas; we as parents would gain nothing by saying 'no' to this request, yet our child learned so much from our encouragement for her do this. She learnt that some societal expectations do not count, that she can challenge the norm and that we will have her back if and when others challenge her. She learnt that her voice, feelings and desires are more important to her than those around her. She developed her sense of self-worth and recognised that her opinion matters. She learnt that self-advocacy could lead to positive outcomes and the importance of staying true to oneself.

This ability to self-advocate has taken time. Building the habit of self-advocacy takes much longer for some to develop than others, but in moments like the Christmas tree you can see how worthwhile it is. This is a child who has spent many years people-pleasing, masking and fawning for the well-being of others in society at a detriment to herself. To help her, we have pointed out our own mistakes so she could become aware that we are not perfect. We have modelled responses and role played with her, included her in discussions and emphasised the value she brings. We have praised her perspective in conversations, especially when it has been different to ours.

You can support your child to develop self-advocacy skills by encouraging them to check in with their body and address their own needs. Perhaps ask if they feel discomfort, or if they are content. Express when you feel uncomfortable yourself so they can learn how to do the same. Model healthy advocating and the setting of boundaries. An opportunity to do this could be if you are walking together in the street when a group of people appears causing it to feel busy. You can openly model that you are choosing to cross to the other side of the street because you will feel more comfortable where it is quieter.

Teach your child how to respectfully disagree with other people and set boundaries for their own safety. Teach that it's okay to leave an environment or people who make you uncomfortable; that they do not need to justify or answer to anyone. Remind them of the non-negotiable of keeping yourself safe and discuss ways in which they could safely leave environments. If your child indicates to you that they are done in an environment honour this and praise them; your child needs to know their discomfort is enough reason to leave. Recently we were on a routine dentist visit. Our child has been able to attend the dentist for a few years, but on this particular occasion the dentist seemed rushed and was constantly talking to our child, giving her direction after direction with no processing time. The dentist did not listen when I asked them to slow down and give my child a minute, so as they gave the next direction, my child firmly told the dentist to 'SSSSHHHH.' The dentist's response was to say she could not speak to them like that and if my child could just lay down, they could start the check-up. My child stood up from the chair and told me we were done. I did not cajole her or ask her to try again. We left. I praised my child for listening to their body and advocating for themself. Once home I rang the dentist to ensure our next visit would have a better outcome and ensured my child's needs would be met in future.

Teaching your child about their personal space is another thing that will help your children to develop self-advocacy. It may be helpful to visually show personal space to your child; you can ask them to hold their arms outwards and draw a circle in the air with their fingertips around themselves. Explain to them that this is their personal space and that everyone has this space around them. You can teach them how to respect personal space by modelling in your interactions with them that you ask for consent to enter their personal space. Reassure your child that you will stand firm with them if other people do not respect their 'no'. An example of this may be when someone in your social circle leaves and asks them for a hug or a kiss goodbye. Encourage your child to say 'No' if they do not want to do this. Explain to the person involved that you are modelling respect for personal body space and allowing your child to set their boundaries.

It may be helpful to spend time discussing some different scenarios where consent may be required. Role play and model that it's ok to scream and gain attention from others if this consent is not asked for. Encourage your child to ask for consent before entering other people's personal space. In our home we give hugs often, but we ask for a hug and respect the decision of the other person. Our child enjoys her back being tickled in a particular manner, she will roll on to her front and indicate she wants me to do this for her. Each and every time I still make sure I ask her, does she want me to tickle her back? I do not touch until she has answered; until I have consent. Our children will often prefer that we cuddle under blankets with them, we ask for consent and discuss what to do if anyone tried getting under the covers that they did not want there. Your child needs these things teaching explicitly to them. They need to understand that they can place boundaries and say 'No' and that if their 'no' is not accepted, they can do more to protect themselves without repercussion.

Clearly teach your child the difference between secrets and surprises. Surprises include other people, have an end point and are intended to create feelings of happiness. Parties, presents, days out are examples of surprises. Secrets have no end point, they exclude other people and keeping hold of them creates feelings of discomfort and sadness. When your child is given a secret and told not to share with anyone, they bear the responsibility of keeping it, they are aware that voicing the secret could create uproar or consequences. When your child has this understanding teach them how to advocate in scenarios when they may be asked to keep a secret. Reassure them they can always come to you with no consequence, that even if the person creating the secret is a friend or family member it's okay to speak to you. Let them know you are there to help them figure if it's a secret or a surprise. Create a circle of safety for your child. These are adults your child feels they can voice concerns to. Make this a visual, draw a circle on paper and write or place a photo of your child in the centre. Place photos or write the names of the adults inside the circle, discuss with your child topics they may share with their circle; school, bullying, consent, homelife, you could write these topics in the circle in a different colour. Outside the circle you could write topics they could discuss with friends or other adults not in their circle, for example; fun activities, meals they have enjoyed, their interests. Let the trusted adults know they form your child's circle of safety and the actions they should take if your child voiced something to them. Stress the importance that the adults act on your child's experience and, at the very least, let you know the child has spoken to them.

The skills for self-advocating within their friendships are also important to develop. Teach your child it's okay to end friendships or create distance if these friendships are no longer bringing them happiness and comfort. Model and role play how they can set these boundaries. Be careful to not praise your child for tolerating discomfort, accepting mistreatment or ignoring their needs for the benefit of other people. Fostering your child's abilities to set boundaries and advocate for their needs to be met is crucial for their well-being and personal safety throughout life. A child who is empowered to assert boundaries will develop a sense of assertiveness and self-respect that can protect and enable them to navigate social situations with confidence. Your child needs to know they can listen to their instincts, trust their own judgement and make choices that prioritise their wellbeing. Your child will learn this from you. By allowing autonomy, advocating for your child and teaching them the skills to self-advocate, you will successfully navigate the complexities of the world together. Your relationship will flourish because of the mutual respect you create as your child learns that their voice counts.

# 3.4 - BE WISE AND THRIVE

Your child will not just arrive at adulthood one day with all the skills they require to live successfully; these skills are taught over time and will develop at their pace. It is the same for you as a parent; the skills you have gradually develop as your knowledge and experience increase.

Through our journey together you have learned how to create the four cornerstones within your home that will consistently support your family and create your safe space. You have discovered how to become your favourite of version of you and place boundaries to protect and support your family in ways that only your family need.

You have been shown how you can **'Be WISE'** in any situation that is not supporting your child effectively. Equipped with this approach you will be able to find the 'why' that will enable you to gain an understanding of the factors that influence your child's responses and adapt your parenting effectively to create an environment that nurtures your child.

You know how to help your child flourish. You have been guided in how you can support your child consistently and effectively in any of the nervous system states by following the **THRIVE** approach. You have been encouraged to advocate for other people to do the same for your child. As you see the relationship between you strengthen, you will realise your child is learning from the greatest teacher that they can have (yes that's you!) that self-advocacy is a tool of strength and that having the courage to act will protect and empower them.

It will be a continuous learning journey for your family; the cornerstones will need to be reviewed, there will be times you forget to be **WISE**, there will be times you wonder if there has been any change. In these moments stop and reflect. Look at where you were. Is your life really still chaos quite as often? Consider how your skills have developed, how your knowledge as a family has increased, how the boundaries you have placed protect and empower you and the steps that you have taken to support your child. You have the knowledge now to create a home where your autistic child can thrive; to create Your Safe Space.

I am far from the perfect parent; my skills and knowledge are still increasing now as our children age. My parenting ten years ago followed the societal expectations laid down for me by the parenting books I read and those people I surrounded myself with. But those books did not help our family; they were not tailored to neurodivergent families with autistic children. As our children developed, I became aware we needed to do life differently but nothing told me how. I have learnt to create a home where my autistic children thrive. I have developed the courage to act when my children have needed me to advocate. I have been willing to learn from their experiences and to adapt our home to meet their needs. I was lucky to have the professional wisdom to guide me to move on from the societal expectations and look after myself in ways that I could manage within our home. I am not the representation of parenting perfection but each day I do myself proud knowing I am being the best parent I can be for our children.

When my children were young there were plenty of occasions I could not manage to take them out on my own, either we would not go, or I would need help from someone to be able to meet their needs. I dreamt of the day I could take my children out on my own, to be able to support them in various environments and not rely on other people to assist us. That day came a long time ago when I learnt to be **WISE,** but the occasion that really sticks in my mind as the one where I truly knew that my children thrive, came quite recently on a cold October night. The children had decided they wanted to see Taylor Swift's concert being shown at the local cinema and they wanted to be there on the opening night. I booked the particular, familiar seats, end of the back row, four seats for the 3 of us so we did not have strangers sat near. The children spent all week making replica Taylor Swift fan bracelets. There were lots of times the excitement became too overwhelming and intrusive thoughts started to creep in; what if after all of this we couldn't make it? Throughout the week we needed to restore the balance and work through the 'what ifs.' I had to be innovative in my planning, there were so many factors and needs to consider that could easily ruin this experience for them. My children are like chalk and cheese; one needs a slow pace whereas the other lives in the moment. I had friends on standby to collect one child if they were done, so the other could stay if needed. The day of the concert was spent with eager anticipation and preparation. Thinking about the environment scared me; I knew the cinema would be full and was apprehensive about the outcome of this event, but the children appeared aware of each other's needs and had each other's back.

It often feels like our children merely survive through life. It's like society is constantly trying to push them as square pegs into a round hole, but that night was a bright shining glimmer of hope. That night, I saw my children stood at the front of a crowded cinema singing and dancing along to Taylor Swift, one with the crowd of all the other young people. I finally knew that I really was helping them to thrive. I thought my heart might burst; relief came from the joyous tears that silently dropped down my cheeks.

The moment didn't end there though. As the concert showing finished, my children eager to be the first out of their seats, ran to the front of the auditorium. They greeted complete strangers as they left, handing out the bracelets they had spent the week making. My faith in society was slightly restored as these strangers accepted the bracelets, stopping and talking to my children, asking which song they enjoyed the most and validating their experience. As the last bracelets were handed over, I reflected on the moment. This was proof that when your child feels safe and secure, we can never say never.

Parenting is a never-ending journey. If your child seeks you out for comfort and care, if you attempt daily to let them know they are supported, valued and loved, if you respond with compassion and let your child know it's okay more often than you don't, then I want you to know you are doing great. You are being the best parent you can be for them right now.

It is up to you what happens from here; you can **'Be WISE and THRIVE',** you can put this book on a shelf to collect dust, you can keep coming back to it and establish the cornerstones one by one, or you can go all out and follow each chapter at the same time. Whatever you do from this moment, do it for you.

Do it for your family.

Do life differently but do it in a way that allows you all to thrive and know that you always have Your Safe Space to return to.

# Wisdom Is Not Just About Knowing What To Do, It's About Having The Courage To Act, The Willingness To Learn And The Endurance To Thrive Amongst The Chaos.

# FINAL THOUGHTS

I want to take a moment to thank you for trusting me to provide you with knowledge that you may have not yet had. For coming on this journey with me and for your commitment to making your home a safe space for your autistic child to thrive. My vision for the future is that every parent is given this book. For those at the start of their journey, as they query if their child is autistic, that society does not make them wait on lists with no support but gives them the information in this book as a roadmap. For those who have been on the journey and feel a little lost, I hope they are given this book to encourage a new way of supporting their child. For those who already have a safe space, I hope they read this book and feel the empowerment that comes with knowing they are helping their child to thrive. Most of all, my vision is that as parents we stand together and spread the word that there is a tribe out there who do life differently, waiting to support us all, to guide us and to show us that our children can thrive.
Much Love Jo G. x

# ABOUT THE AUTHOR

*Jo Gaunt*

Based in the north of England, Jo is a neurodivergent advocate who collaborates with neurodivergent individuals to create safe spaces for them to thrive. She has over 20 years' experience working alongside autistic and other neurodivergent individuals within a variety of home and educational settings. Jo has a BPhil degree in Special Educational Needs - Autism and has used this expertise to develop and teach strategies to both education staff and parents, with the aim of developing their understanding of emotional regulation, the nervous system and neurodiversity. She has assisted young people to explore and understand their neurodivergence in positive ways whilst accepting their unique way of being.

Despite Jo's extensive professional knowledge, her parental journey echoes that of many parents. As a parent to three neurodivergent children she has had to defend unconventional approaches, faced dismissal from a variety of professionals and has struggled against the endless bureaucratic barriers in the search for necessary support.

Over the past decade, Jo has assisted her family to confirm and embrace their neurodivergence. The whole family is a mix of autistic, attention/hyperactive*, dyslexic and sensory divergent, with a pervasive drive for autonomy*. Jo's professional background has provided her with a clear insight into successful strategies and support for autistic individuals, but it is her lived experience as a mum and wife in a neurodivergent family that she credits to giving her the knowledge and experience she needed to create a safe space where everyone can thrive.

To support other families Jo facilitates a neurodivergent-affirming community, 'Breathe' for parents and carers of autistic and neurodivergent individuals to meet, chat and develop supportive strategies surrounded by other people who understand.

This book is a result of so many families expressing to Jo that her innovative methods have had a positive impact on their own family space. Jo's vision is that no family will feel as alone as she did at the start of her journey in creating her own safe space.

To connect with Jo and find out how to work with her. You can visit her website at www.JoGaunt.com here you will find information about her socials, free resources and the details for the parent community 'Breathe'.

In the event that you notice any amendments that need to be made within the book, for example inaccurate references please make contact via Jo's website.

* Attention/Hyperactive also known as ADHD, attention deficit hyperactivity disorder.
* Pervasive drive for autonomy also known as PDA, pathological demand avoidance.

Printed in Great Britain
by Amazon